CLOSED FILE

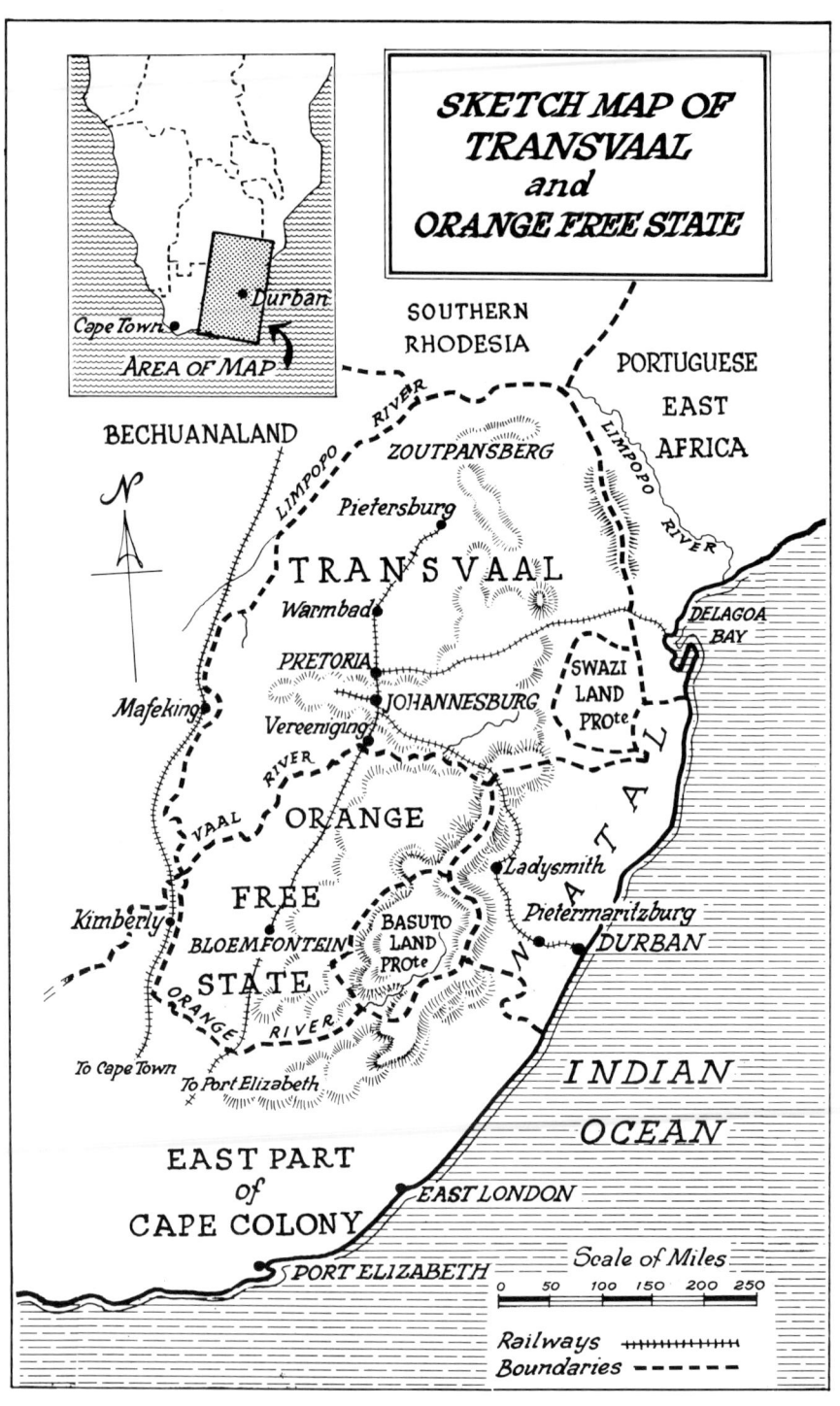

Map of the general war area in the Transvaal and the Orange Free State

CLOSED FILE

Kit Denton

RIGBY

Other books by Kit Denton

A Walk Around My Cluttered Mind
The Breaker
The Thinkable Man
Gallipoli Illustrated

This is for three of my closest friends —
my children; Jo, Andrew, and Phillipa

National Library of Australia
Cataloguing-in-Publication entry

Denton, Kit.
　Closed file.
　ISBN 0 7270 1739 x.
　1. Morant, Breaker, 1865–1902. 2. South African
　War, 1899–1902. 3. Trials (Military offences)—
　South Africa. I. Title.

968.04′8

RIGBY PUBLISHERS • ADELAIDE
SYDNEY • MELBOURNE • BRISBANE • PERTH
NEW YORK • LONDON • AUCKLAND
First published 1983
Copyright © 1983 Kit Denton
All rights reserved
Typeset in Australia
Printed by Everbest Printing Co. Ltd, Hong Kong

Acknowledgments

The search for information about The Breaker and the people and events of his times has been a long one. It started for me in 1970 and there are still gaps to be filled but, thanks to the help I have had with this book, they are smaller and fewer now.

For their personal recollections and pictures I am grateful to Roy Witton, the Lenehan family, Mr W. P. Walters, and the people of Tenterfield—especially Win Percival, John Dearden, and Noelle McKellow and Ken Halliday of the *Tenterfield Star*. For permission to use private papers and correspondence my thanks go to Mr R. H. Colless, Len Brown, Miss C. N. Jennings, Mrs Eleanor McLaren, and the delightful Miss Hilda Truman of Adelaide. Theo Barker in Bathurst and the Most Reverend T. T. Reed in Adelaide were the sources of important information and Jules Zanetti, of *People* magazine, and Lt.-Col. David Brown, Army Public Relations, were both good enough to pass usable material to me.

In South Africa the editor of *Historia* freely gave his permission for me to quote from that respected journal and the late Dr W. H. J. Punt and Dr Dick Schulenberg sent me photographs and archival papers which have been of extraordinary value. Some of those papers needed translation from the Afrikaans, and for that long and hard work I am indebted to Dr Tony Pohl, now of Adelaide.

The Registrars of the Scottish Record Office in Edinburgh and of Births and Deaths in Sydney, and Alan Wilkes, Archivist in the University of New England, all made my task easier. My thanks, also, to Mr B. F. Clayton, Australian Army (Retired), for his invaluable help with a most difficult piece of procedural research—and to the many people who rang me with snippets of information and whose names are legion!

Major-General Sir David Hughes-Morgan, Bt., C.B.E., is Director of Legal Services at the Ministry of Defence in London, and to him and that ministry go my sincere gratitude for friendly help and for permission to quote from letters and documents. At the Australian War Memorial in Canberra unstinting aid and interest from Jan Mulqueen and Michael Piggott made it possible for me to find and use papers and photographs which are crucial to this book. In London, John Abbott and Diana Birch were of great help, and Dorothea Rose of Illustration Research Service has been a tower of strength. I am grateful also to the Honourable Stephen Loch of London for allowing me to use material drawn from the record of Loch's Horse, and so make it possible to flesh out some rather thin bones of knowledge.

My special thanks are reserved for Stella Guthrie and her husband Copper in Adelaide, for their long-continued interest, active help, and unreserved hospitality; and for my dear friend Maggie Swifte who did all the typing from some pretty horrible roughs of mine. Her husband, Lt.-Col. Tim Swifte, Retired, was quick with information and picked up a number of my errors. Lastly, I am most grateful to my daughter Phillipa for all her help, especially with the index.

I would also like to thank Angus & Robertson Publishers for permission to reproduce the photograph of Lieutenant George Ramsdale Witton which appears on page 54. This photograph appears in *Scapegoats of the Empire: The True Story of the Breaker Morant's Bushveldt Carbineers* by George Witton originally published 1907 and reprinted by Angus & Robertson in 1982. This photograph of Witton was taken on his departure from Portland Prison.

Contents

Foreword   9

CIRCUMSTANCES   11
CRIMES   39
CRUCIFIED   46
   Picton   52
   Witton   54
   Lenehan   57
   Thomas   61
   Handcock   64
   Morant   68
COURT MARTIAL   85
CONSEQUENCES   117
   Picton   129
   Witton   130
   Lenehan   134
   Thomas   145

Select Bibliography   158
Index   159

Foreword

The name 'Breaker Morant' is evocative, linked nowadays with the images conjured up in my novel and in the film based on the episodes leading to the man's death. That those images are, as often as not, very wrong seems less important than that they exist as a focus of interest. The top-dressing of dramatic licence and literary colouring together with the watering of popular misconceptions have produced a fine green lawn to pleasure the eye and to encourage relaxation of thought; very few people choose to believe that there is stony and uncomfortable ground just below the bright grass.

In that inhospitable subsoil lie the rocks of vicious warfare, international politics, and dubious military-legal practice, and between the rocks writhe the worms of doubt and speculation. I have to confess to having provided food for those worms—but then I was fed myself on a rather strange diet of double-talk, half-truths, and part-facts. Some came from people in Australia.

The old and angry man who had served with Morant in the 2nd South Australian Mounted Infantry and who first told me about him spun a splendid yarn which was the truth as he remembered it about the man in Australia and in the first part of his Boer War life. But the rest of the story, the part about the Bush Veldt Carbineers, that was hearsay, rumour, and speculation—but it was fed to me as truth and I accepted it as such.

When I began to follow the story through, conversations with other old people and press reports of the time gave me no immediate cause to suspect what I had first been told. The emphasis was always the same: that The Breaker and his mates had been railroaded by the British; that Kitchener was the villain of the piece; and that the Government in London had made a sacrifice of Australians as a piece of political expediency to soothe ruffled German emotions.

And then, in London, when I tried to find substantial proof of what had really happened, tried to find documentation, I was met with bland denials that *anything* untoward had taken place and with a variety of explanations for the absence of the transcripts of court martial proceedings. These ranged from 'they were loaned out and not returned' through 'we don't have them but the Navy/Army/Public Records Office/Prime Minister's Office have them', the variations depending on who was answering my query at the time. Within one week I was told at the Public Records Office that the papers 'should be here somewhere' and that 'they were destroyed by enemy action during the war'.

Six weeks of that sort of thing left me with the strong belief that what I had been told in Australia was so; that the British were, indeed, covering up. As a writer with a novel in mind it seemed to me to be excellent material on which to base a major theme in the story I was going to tell. So my book did much to perpetuate the weeds in the garden of that rocky and worm-laden subsoil.

In the long years since the firing-party's shots rang out in South Africa that under-soil has slipped and subsided in places so that, while the lawn above has more recently sprung greener and lusher, the hollows in it have become a little deeper—and in those hollows lie the plants which once flowered as The Breaker did. These were the other men concerned in and with his story; in and with his life and times and death. Because of The Breaker's more vivid colours those men are seen less distinctly and, indeed, are often overlooked entirely.

The Breaker was the man who used the name Harry Harbord Morant. Executed with him was Peter Joseph Handcock. Arrested and tried with them were George Ramsdale Witton and Harry Picton. Suspected and deeply affected by that trial and its consequences was Robert William Lenehan. Most deeply affected, for the rest of his life, was James Francis Thomas.

Because the romantic story is an entity, it is easy to forget that all those men had separate lives, unconnected with one another, and that for all but two of them those lives went on after Morant and Handcock were shot and buried. Outside the confines of the story, of the film, there were beginnings before The Beginning—and there were certainly continuations after The End. I suppose if we want to look at the whole logic of the thing the real beginning was in the middle of the seventeenth century.

1

Circumstances

When, in 1652, the Dutch East India Company established a station at the Cape of Good Hope it was for the logical reason that it lay conveniently along the line of passage between The Netherlands and the outposts from which they were drawing commodities and wealth.

Over the next century-and-a-half The Cape flourished, not only as a way-station but also as a refuge to which fled men and families and whole groups of people escaping the religious pressures placed on them in their homelands. From Holland, from France, from Germany they came — Calvinists, Huguenots, Lutherans, Protestants; after them came, inevitably, the traders and merchants and drifters; around them grew settlements, towns, and cities and beyond them farms and vineyards.

Because of the nature of those first and following incomers there was always a peculiar strength about the place; the strength which comes from a deep and abiding faith, the conviction of a close tie with God, and which then grows and becomes more profound from the struggle to tear a living from untouched soil, to create a New World. By the start of the nineteenth century the people of The Cape were tough, individualistic, and solidly established, not just on the land but in their attitudes. They regarded themselves as special people, self-sustaining, strong, and in the immediate eye of Heaven for their rigid adherence to their faith.

But by then they knew, and knew well, that they weren't alone in their own earthly Eden. Every time they moved outwards, every time a farmer started clearing land, every time hunters went out for food, they invaded — for wherever they had settled was the age-old land of the tribes, the people of Africa Primordial, and the long years saw a continuing striving, the white men moving inexorably inland,

Stephanus Johannes Paulus Kruger ('Oom Paul'), Boer President from 1883 to 1902. He defeated the Jameson Raid in 1895

the black men resisting each step. To the settlers and their followers the tribesmen were doubly wrong. They dared to delay the expansion and progress of the incomers, and that was not to be tolerated; and they were black and heathen, the sons of Ham, cursed by The Book to be the servants of servants. That they should resist men who were not only white and Christian but *the* true Christians, this was a transgression against both God and man!

So by 1800 the white men of The Cape were entrenched: physically on the land; socially in tight family and neighbour-groups; and religiously within the confines of a rigid and fundamentalist belief. The land was theirs and the black people of the land were there to be killed when they fought and enslaved when they did not. Theirs was an insular, inward-looking world.

Out beyond them there were tidal waves of action, set into world-sweeping motion by the small man called Napoleon Bonaparte. Where the Dutch had seen the Cape of Good Hope as their way-station to the East Indies the British suddenly recognised its strategic importance to them in the light of Napoleon's martial ambitions — the sea-lanes to the colonies of New Zealand and Australia and, much more important, to the treasure-house of India, lay past The Cape. It suddenly seemed to England that the southern tip of Africa, inhabited by a scattering of Europeans, ought properly to be a place in which to establish a Royal Navy base and, with the chilling lack of consideration of the world's strongest navy, England simply moved in and annexed the territory.

'Annexed' was then, as it is now, the formal word for 'took', in the sense of stealing. The English who went to The Cape then saw little if anything to recommend it beyond its plain first purpose as a naval base and a safe port for trade ships. The interior held nothing of great import for them and, although migration was encouraged, the leakage of British settlers inland was slow and small. But it happened and by 1814 when the Dutch, willy-nilly, signed a treaty formally yielding the territory, there were three clear groupings there: the descendants of the old settlers, the ones who were calling themselves 'Afrikaners'; the native tribes, both those living and working under the whites and those still living freely on the border edges and beyond; and the British — the 'Uitlanders', the foreigners. The seeds were planted for the growth of a garden of weeds.

Twenty years later there was an unmistakably British atmosphere about The Cape; among the old Dutch buildings had sprung up solidly English stonework. Overlaying the wash of native tongues there were two languages spoken in the streets, but there was only one spoken in the rooms where policy was enacted and laws made —

Boer General Christiaan De Wet later held office in the South African Government
(*Photo: Australian War Memorial*)

and it was in that English that the London-made laws were promulgated in 1834 which emancipated slaves in all parts of the Empire (and that included the Cape Colony).

The constantly growing resentment of the Afrikaners at once had a focus. The British, a minority to the Afrikaners as they themselves were to the Africans, had usurped their land, brought in new systems, a different language, and a lax approach to religion. Now they were with one move taking away their God-given right to own slaves and, in freeing the blacks, opening the way to economic change and possible physical danger.

More and more of them decided to leave, seeing no way to live as they wished in such a system, and 1835 saw the start of the Great Trek northwards, a move out of the British sphere of influence, across the Orange River to found the Orange Free State and, for some, the further move north over the Vaal River to establish the South African Republic. The move out went on for years. The first migrants (the Voortrekkers) followed by hundreds of others; whole families with their possessions and cattle, their dogs and guns and servants, rolling away across the veldt and across the rivers to live as they wished. The desire took no heed of the fact that they, too, were invading—as their forefathers had done—the homelands of proud native tribes.

In 1852, recognising the facts of what had happened and with nothing inland to attract them as administrators, the British recognised the independence of the South African Republic; two years later they recognised the Orange Free State. But before doing either of those things Britain annexed Natal. Like the Afrikaners the British had found the natives of the inland to be hostile and spirited fighters—none more so than the Zulu against whom bloody war had been fought. British military pride had been shattered by the massacre of Isandlhwana and restored by the extraordinary stand at Rorke's Drift but, inevitably, the Zulu nation had been defeated as a military power.

The defeat did nothing to stop the clans and tribes from washing their assegais in blood whenever the time seemed ripe. The blood was impartially Afrikaner and British and the annexation of Natal, lying across Zululand, made for an effective bulwark. It also placed the British neatly between the two Afrikaner states and the sea so that the Afrikaners then had native tribes to their north and west and the British to their south and east, and they had no access to a seaboard except through territory that was not their own.

Differences of opinion and attitude became of less importance in the face of the new problem raised in the late 1860s when a pipe of

The Boer General Jacobus Herkulaas De la Rey. When the first World War erupted he organised a Boer rebellion but was killed before it began (*Photo: Australian War Memorial*)

diamonds was found in the Orange Free State. For the first time the disregarded land held promise, offered an attraction to Britain and to the explorer-exploiters who had always carried the Empire outwards. Five years after the discovery Britain, having long recognised the State's independence, calmly annexed it and, six years after that, took over the South African Republic. That time, though, they met resistance. The men who were by then calling themselves 'Boers', a word meaning 'farmers', fought back, fought hard, and won. At the Battle of Majuba Hill a British column of more than 600 men, posted on the hill's summit, was attacked and driven off, losing a third of their number killed and wounded, fifty taken prisoner, and their commander killed. The defeat at Majuba led to an armistice and the end of what was, properly speaking, the First Boer War. That was in 1881. Five years after that gold was found in the South African Republic, the area the British called the Transvaal, and, as happened in California, in the Yukon, and in Australia the lure of it dragged miners and prospectors and hopeful diggers into the land, and they came predominantly from Britain and her colonies. Within two or three years the tensions which built up had become close to unbearable.

It is easy to see the causes of the Boer bitterness. They had seen ancestral lands taken over at The Cape and their rights denied them; they had left, determined to found a new land, and they had fought distance and danger and done just that, only to have it taken away again. They had struck back and won a just fight and found themselves the owners of the commodity which could make them fully independent and a power in the world—and then discovered themselves in the position of owning a land in which they were rapidly becoming twice a minority; outnumbered by the black population, which they held in subjugation, and in danger of being swamped by an inrush of largely-British whites who were hungry for riches. The one way in which they could hope to exert their own form of control was politically, and they legislated against the incomers to deny them political rights and power.

They had reckoned without the magnetic strength of gold, the irresistible pull of the metal for men of massive ambition. Such a man was Cecil Rhodes, an Englishman who went to work in the Kimberley diamond mines as a young man and made a fortune within three years. By 1881, using his undoubted business genius and a ruthless flair for getting what he wanted, he had established a combine which took in most of the Kimberley mines and controlled almost all of the world's diamond production. In that year he was elected to the Cape Colony Assembly and began the task of spreading

Later to become Field-Marshal Smuts and Prime Minister of South Africa, when this picture was taken Jan Christiaan Smuts was only thirty and already a skilled Boer general (*Photo: Australian War Memorial*)

British influence throughout South Africa, realising at the outset that such authority could only be gained at the expense of both the native population and the Afrikaners. By the time he became Premier of Cape Colony in 1890 Rhodes had forced the annexation of Bechuanaland (now Botswana) and enforced the surrender by the Matabele of their homeland to Britain. Known now as Zimbabwe, that great stretch of land was then called Rhodesia. His ambition, though, was for Britain to control *all* of South Africa and the building tensions in the Transvaal, the power of the gold there, the great numbers of British on the goldfields, prompted him to inspire an uprising there against the Boers. The impetus for the rising was to be an attack by Rhodesians, led by Doctor Leander Jameson, against the Transvaal. It was poorly planned and executed and the expected support from within was never forthcoming. As a military/political manoeuvre it was a fiasco. It was the end of Rhodes as a leader in the land and he resigned his Premiership.

For four years attempts were made to patch up the increasing rift between British and Boer, but the differences were too great and the Jameson raid provided a constant goad—to the British it was a reminder of their ineffectual control of the situation; to the Boers a reminder of their strong position, morally, and, because of their gold, economically.

At the political level the Republic's President, Paul Kruger, led a government which had no intention, no matter what it said, of allowing franchise rights to Uitlanders and so to yield power to them. Kruger and his party—and the Boer population at large— were as rigid in attitude as their forefathers who had fled Europe and entered the wilderness rather than endure a change in their beliefs. To them the British were still, and always would be, interlopers, and there was always the hope that Boers still in Cape Colony and in Natal would support any move made against the British; just as it was hoped that there would be intervention by foreign powers with no love for Britain—France, Germany, even America. So the long months of discussion and negotiation in which Britain attempted to extract rights for the Uitlanders from the Boers spun away in growing rancour and fears grew that action would replace talk. Uitlander families began to reverse the Great Trek and to move south from Pretoria, where feeling against them was growing. Six thousand troops were sent from India to Durban in September of 1899 and the Government of the Orange Free State at once announced that if war should come between Britain and Boer their State would support the Transvaal no matter what the cost.

Suddenly a time of confrontation had come and Boer troops

Possibly the most military-looking picture of a Boer general, General Louis Botha (seated second from left) and his staff meet with Kitchener and his staff at an abortive peace conference in 1900. Botha was South African Prime Minister 1910–19 (*Photo: Australian War Memorial*)

moved out to their borders. An ultimatum was delivered to the British Government stipulating terms which would have been virtually impossible to meet, and stating that non-compliance with those terms by 5 p.m. on 11 October 1899 would constitute a formal declaration of war.

Two-and-a-quarter years after the start of the Second Boer War, Peter Handcock and Breaker Morant were executed.

*   *   *   *

So the fighting began and the news of it was followed eagerly in Britain and in the colonies, where by the turn of the year men began to volunteer for the Colours.

The turn of that year of 1899 was significant for with it came Black Week, a week in which Britain's military pride was humbled. On

10 December at Stormberg, the next day at Magersfontein, and four days after that at Colenso, the pomp and power of the British Army was defeated by South African farmers—and even more humble pie was served out within the month by yet another crashing defeat at Spion Kop.

By then Australians were in the fight. A contingent of New South Wales Lancers, professional soldiers and the senior Australian cavalry regiment, was training at Aldershot for a military tournament and they went straight out to The Cape, attached to the 9th Lancers and seeing action at the battle of the Modder River towards the end of December.

Soon other contingents were being formed, not only in Australia but also in Canada, India, New Zealand, Natal, and the Cape Colony itself, and it soon became clear that they were going to be needed. Sir Redvers Buller, the Commander of the South African forces, was enormously popular with his men and even his reverses did nothing to hide the fact that he cared greatly for the welfare of his troops. The trouble was that there were too many reverses and, as it became more

Below left: The Undress uniform of the Orange Free State Artillery at the time of the outbreak of the war. *Below right:* The Full Dress helmet of the Orange Free State Artillery. It is leather and brass with an orange and white plume and the State crest (*Photos: Australian War Memorial*)

The heliograph was used widely in South Africa where the open spaces and bright sunshine made conditions ideal for that type of signalling (*Photo: Australian War Memorial*)

and more obvious that the General's mode of warfare was too static, too out-dated to cope with the sort of mobile and adaptable enemy he faced, so a new commander was appointed — and given more and still more troops.

Parallels between the Boer War and the Viet Nam campaign are sometimes irresistible. Disregarding the political and economic factors, and sticking to the military level, in both cases a large and massively-equipped Army fought civilian-soldiers on their familiar home-ground, fought people who wore no uniforms, used unorthodox tactics, and had the aid and comfort of the populace around them. In both cases the terrain and the tactics of their enemies led the Army commanders, schooled in other sorts of warfare, first to increase their forces greatly in an attempt to overwhelm the opposition, and then to modify the nature of their forces while establishing a pattern of attempted enclosure and great destruction. It has also been suggested often enough that the cases of Breaker Morant and his companions were early versions of that of Lieutenant Calley and his companions—that orders were given and followed, even though they were savage orders. The principal difference is that Calley wasn't executed.

In 1899, when hostilities began in South Africa, neither the British troops there nor their commanders saw any reason to believe that the actions they were to engage in would be in any major sense out of the ordinary. Out of the understood *military* ordinary, that is. The second half of the century which was ending had seen the first of the modern wars, the wars in which a whole new range of personal and remote weapons were used for the first time and in which the effective use of railways for troop movement and supply had been demonstrated. The American Civil War and the Franco-Prussian War had, between them, seen the death of old-style campaigning, but it was a demise which British arms refused to recognise and they

A group of officers showing the diversity of uniforms; the two on the right in the back row are 'University Volunteer Rifles' (*Photo: Australian War Memorial*)

went into the Boer War carrying with them the dead weight of their past.

In that half-century they had fought in the Crimea, had put down the Indian Mutiny, and defeated the Zulu, and they had done those things in a fashion that they still saw as good enough. Certainly there had been some changes and modifications to weapons, equipment, and uniforms, but the changes in attitude were less apparent. The man who had been an eighteen-year-old subaltern in the Crimea was at the start of his sixties when the Boer War began and might well have been commanding a regiment of troops on active service, or been a Member of Parliament or a senior Civil Servant exercising some influence on the conduct of a campaign. Even the younger men, those expectably of Field rank, had been brought up in a national atmosphere of success at arms against Maoris, Indians, Burmese, and Africans—and in a service in which ceremonial and social life was at least as important as efficient soldiering.

An officer's position in society and the size of his bank balance were considered good indications of his fitness to command; his wealth and breeding generally dictated whether he went into one of the 'better' regiments or not. Whatever his regiment or his military rank his actual knowledge of the arts and sciences of martial life took second place behind the social requirements of the day and his men were, generally, managed and taught by the non-commissioned officers. Even then the amount of actual training for active-service conditions ran to less than sixty days in any year, the bulk of the soldier's life being spent on ceremonial and guard duties, in keeping his gear and uniform in a suitably-impressive parade state, or carrying out the sort of household, garden, and stable tasks which his officers expected of a staff of servants.

When military drills *were* undertaken the stress was on rigidly-disciplined formations, massed, straight-line advances, volley-fire, and all the other tactics which had proved effective enough against Napoleon and the Russians. Yet there were clear enough instructions laid down by Sir Garnet Wolseley, the Commander-in-Chief. In the foreword to the Infantry Drill Manual of 1896 he wrote, 'General and other officers commanding are enjoined to devote their utmost attention to carrying out the system of training, drill and manoeuvre . . . the aim of which is to obtain, at the decisive moment, the greatest development of infantry fire under the most careful supervision and control. To secure this a thorough training is essential . . .' It may have been essential but it was seldom given.

Not that the Boer fighting-man had, in the main, any formal training. In the years before the war began the Kruger government had been able to put some of its gold to useful work and had bought some excellent artillery from Krupp in Germany and from Creusot in France, and had well-trained gunners. The Republic certainly had the Royal Artillery outgunned in the first part of the war, just as its troops had Britain's at a disadvantage with its rifles.

Britain still had a few units armed with the Martini-Henry 1871 rifle, a single-shot weapon, and the first of the magazine rifles, the Lee-Metford and Lee-Enfield, were still unfamiliar in some regiments. The Boer fighting-man was well armed with Mauser and Mannlicher and Winchester rifles, and was very familiar with them, just as he was accustomed to using them expertly. Where a man lived many kilometres away from regular supplies and depended on hunting game in order to feed his family, he learned when he was very young to make every shot count, whether he was firing on foot or hidden behind a low bush or in the saddle.

There was another salient difference—the Tommy Atkins of the day was marched into battle, carefully positioned, and advanced almost in Review Order. During the march-up he would be carrying a fair amount of weight over his conspicuously-coloured tunic, scarlet and crossed with white, pipe-clayed belts, topped with a white, brass-spiked solar topi. Behind him would come, under a

This is 'Long Cecil', used by the Boers during the siege of Kimberley and probably bought from Krupp (*Photo: Australian War Memorial*)

This Boer gun appears to be a 10- or 12-pounder similar to American and French models. The gun team's rifles look like a Mauser, two British Lee-Metfords, and two Danish-type carbines (*Photo: Australian War Memorial*)

cloud of dust observable for kilometres, the supply and baggage train of wagons—and watching it all from concealed positions the Boers would lie in wait, the horses on which they had ridden held behind them, their ordinary clothes merging with the terrain, the heat and dust and space all familiar to them. And they knew they could hit their targets at ranges close to 1.5 kilometres.

Both sides had the newest infantry weapon, too, the Maxim machine-gun, capable of inflicting awful damage when properly used. Perhaps it was that weapon which most clearly defined the essential differences between the two forces, for the British system of rigid and formalised manoeuvre of very visible bodies of troops was vulnerable to fast and accurate fire, while the Boer method of concealment, attack, and a swift withdrawal gave them the maximum protection from it.

At the outset, British arms in South Africa mustered something like 10 000 men with a long, seaborne supply-line behind them. There were more than 80 000 names on the Boer commando lists with a likely 50 000 of them ready for action—mounted, self-equipped, and very adequately armed.

Lord Roberts of Kandahar, Victoria Cross winner in the Indian Mutiny, sailed for South Africa two days before Christmas 1899 to take command of the forces there. He had just lost his son at Colenso and was heavy with grief, but some of his load was lightened when he was joined by the officer who had been appointed his Chief of Staff — Horatio Herbert Kitchener, the man who had retaken Khartoum from the Mahdi and avenged the death of General Gordon. Kitchener of Khartoum, two years later, would sign the death warrants of Harry Morant and Peter Handcock.

By the spring of 1901 the war was practically over. That, at any rate, was the voiced opinion of Lord Roberts and he was right in one sense at least. The formal part *was* indeed at an end, the part of the war which saw all the set-piece battles fought, which saw the sieges and their lifting and the confrontations between apparent field forces on both sides. So by winter's end Roberts felt able to declare with confidence that the war was won. He was, of course, drastically

Another weapon used by both sides — the Maxim .303 machine-gun. The gunner is a New Zealander (*Photo: Australian War Memorial*)

Lord Roberts of Kandahar commanded the British forces in the Boer War 1899–1900

wrong. Certainly President Kruger had left the scene, escaping into Portuguese territory; General Botha's Boer army was decisively beaten and many of his men had surrendered, swearing not to take up arms again; and the Transvaal had been annexed again. Roberts had initiated a policy of burning Boer farms in order that the enemy's supplies and support should be cut off. He was ready to hand over command and go home to England as a victor.

It says little for his grasp of the situation, or for his imagination, that he discounted or ignored the fact that Botha was still at large, even though his army had lost the field, and that other very efficient Boer commanders were still active—De Wet, De la Rey, and Smuts—as well as close to 40 000 fighting Boers. In fact a new war, a new *kind* of war, was just about to begin with Kitchener the new commander of an army which by now numbered over 200 000 men and in which, for the first time, the enemy was taken to include all civilians within any area of operations.

The Maxim 1-pounder quick-firer, used by both sides with its sound earning it the nickname of 'Pompom' (*Photo: Australian War Memorial*)

Lord Kitchener of Khartoum became Secretary of State for War in 1914

The problem from Kitchener's point of view was that his very sizeable force was anything but a unified command. It is likely that half of it was absorbed in administrative and supply tasks, in guarding lines of communication and garrison areas, and in patrolling possible zones of action without knowing whether the possibility would ever become fact. The rest of the army was scattered around a vast tract of country and it included numbers of colonial volunteers whose time of enlistment was expiring, as well as many units whose unsuitability for the type of warfare involved had been well demonstrated but which were still, to some extent, resistant to change. The lance and the sword were less than effective against concealed and accurate rifle-fire coming from broken and rising terrain, just as there was little value in solid formations and rigid drill-lines against fast, mounted, hit-and-run raiders.

It was this last which now marked the tactics of the Boers in this second and miserable phase; a true guerrilla war had begun with the greening of the veldt in that springtide of 1901. The fresh grasses meant ample food almost anywhere for the Boer horses, and the milder weather made for more comfort in their riders' open campaigning. Those things plus the still-available help from outlying and isolated farms, and ready intelligence from settlement Boers who had daily sight of the British forces, all meant the intensification of harassing attacks and ambushes, of sudden, darting rushes out of false dawns, of flurries of saddleborne rifle-fire and tossed explosives, of the breaking-up of supply columns and the taking of ammunition and supplies and lives. Despite a number of reverses 1901 began with the Boers in invisible occupation of huge stretches of countryside which the British ostensibly had conquered.

In Britain there was the loom of a general election fought largely on the issues of the Boer War; in South Africa Kitchener chafed with the itch to take up the post of Commander-in-Chief in India. The combined pressures led to attempts to end the war as quickly as possible, to bring the Boers to conference and so to peace. Meanwhile the need was paramount to prove that the British had actually won, that they were prepared to confer but only from a position of victorious strength. And so the turkey-shoot began, an almost ritualised system of clearance of the country to force the guerrillas back and away from any source of aid or supply and to partition the cleared land into fortified areas, each with its own garrison forces and with no hindrance from civilian occupants. Kitchener and his staff set out a great grid, moving troops into each square in a planned and methodical fashion, clearing the inhabitants, burning their farms and crops, sullying the wells, stringing barbed

This solid and seemingly-permanent blockhouse formed part of Kitchener's protective system. Its number shows its placement in the great grid of little forts and barbed wire which was established (*Photo: Australian War Memorial*)

wire, and building strategic blockhouses. The echoes came more than half-a-century later when we grew familiar with terms like 'search and destroy' and 'defoliation', just as we had by then recognised the horror implicit in the words 'concentration camp', a term first used for the enclosures into which Boer civilians, most of them women and children, were moved when they were forcibly evacuated from their homes.

It ought to be remembered that the burnings and internments had been started by Roberts, under whom Kitchener served with steadfast loyalty and professionalism. When he took over the command Kitchener faced not simply the political pressure to end the war in a manner satisfactory to Britain but the military pressures of a still-very-active and effective enemy, the dispersal of his forces, heavy losses of horses, and very many of his men either sick or wounded and in hospital or due for demobilisation or engaged in unnecessary duties—unnecessary, that is, as far as *active* service was concerned.

His continuation and expansion of the policy of destruction and removal was logical. If the farms were burnt the women and children on them would be without shelter or sustenance, so they had to be shifted elsewhere; logistics dictated that they be placed together and that, as far as Kitchener was concerned, was that. They were concentrated in large groups in internment camps and at the command level little or no attention was paid to the conditions in those camps. There was fighting to do; the internees were safe out of the way — militarily they now had no importance. But that wasn't the Boer point of view. When word began to spread, first of the camps themselves and then of the increasingly poor conditions in them, the effect was to further fan the flames of resentment, of hatred, among the Boers still in the field, and a cruel war began to assume the proportions of a savage one.

Part of Kitchener's policy was to expand the number of fighting troops available to him. Reinforcements from Britain were almost non-existent by then, regular regiments having exhausted their depots of trained battalions, the flow of volunteers having diminished to a feeble trickle, and the influx of useful men from the colonies providing no more than a counter-balance for the numbers

Most blockhouses were less substantial than the one in the previous picture and were designed to be reasonably strong against light attacks and able to be erected quickly and economically (*Photo: Australian War Memorial*)

Never renowned for their elegance of dress, by 1902 these Australians were hard to distinguish from the Boers (*Photo: Australian War Memorial*)

who, time-expired, were due to return home. An amount of re-recruitment went on, the re-enlisting of men at the end of their service periods, and Kitchener instituted a drive to rout out soldiers in rear echelon and hideaway posts who could be used at the front.

A bitter lesson had been well taught by the Boers and was now seen to have been well-learned by Kitchener and some of his field commanders. It was simply that in that terrain, under those conditions, the Boer method of warfare was vastly more effective than the British. The use of mounted men to move into an area quickly, fight a short and limited action, and ride away just as quickly eliminated the need for heavy baggage and awkward lines of communication.

Kitchener's requirement was for more yeomanry soldiers, for mounted infantry units so that the Boer commandos could be fought by their own methods. It had already been shown that colonial troops of that kind from Canada, New Zealand, and Australia were very good at that sort of warfare—they were largely men who were used to long and hard days in the saddle; men from outdoor

Left: A smart young trooper of the NSW Citizens' Bushmen just prior to embarkation for South Africa. *Below:* A year later the trooper in the previous picture was more likely to look like this member of the 5th South Australian Bushmen (*Photos: Australian War Memorial*)

occupations in places which were often as barren as the rocky uplands above the veldt. They had more in common with the Boers than with the mainly urban and formally-trained British soldiers, and they tended to operate in a much more free-wheeling fashion than many British officers liked. But they had proved their worth and much of the re-enlistment came from among those men, many of the cadres which stiffened newly-raised mounted infantry units were formed from their numbers. By the summer Kitchener had close to a quarter-of-a-million men under command; about 80 000 of them were mounted and half of those riders were colonial troops.

Considering that the Boer forces were by then down to under 50 000, of whom a likely 15 000 were ready and able to fight at any one time, Kitchener's figures look impressive. The truth is that very many of his mounted troops were only partly trained for the work and, despite the inflow of a staggering 10 000 remounts a month, the loss and wastage of horses was a continuing problem. Nonetheless the war was in some ways being taken to the Boers for the first time by their own methods. Standards of dress in the British forces had changed and relaxed to the extent that they were much more a part of

Boer troops in the field—dressed for work, with a variety of weapons, and showing a diversity of age-range (*Photo: Australian War Memorial*)

Camp life on the veldt was usually temporary and never very comfortable (*Photo: Australian War Memorial*)

the countryside when they moved, even if their baggage wagons were no less conspicuous. They tended to operate less as great masses of foot-weary men and more as smaller, mobile, mounted columns.

Those who had been there longest had absorbed lessons in fieldcraft which the Army had not taught them but which the Boers had—the early feeling about fighting 'natives' had become one of respect for the enemy's ability as a fighting man, if not as a proper soldier. The deep-rooted feelings of resentment had not changed, though, even if they were totally different in character. For the British forces the feeling came from a mix of having spent too long in trying to put down an opponent who seemed impossible to crush, no matter how many times he was beaten; of sensing that the civilians among whom they moved and sometimes lived were, in fact, against them passively when observed but actively whenever it was possible; of the knowledge that in England there were strong and growing divisions of opinion about what they were doing in South Africa and of a frequent feeling of outrage at fighting men who often wore captured British uniforms, who sometimes stripped prisoners and sent them back to their own lines naked, who fought with ferocity and a single-mindedness which was at once puzzling and fearsome.

Among the Boers that single-minded attitude was understandably based in the fact that they were fighting on and for their own land, fighting for their homes and livelihood and against an invader. They had nothing to lose by going on with the fight as bitterly as they could against greatly superior numbers and despite open divisions among their own politicians and many of their people. The bitterness deepened and, as the Boers began to suffer from Kitchener's military policies, as their support and supplies began to dwindle, so their actions in the field began to be harsher and the need to arm and equip themselves from the British became more imperative.

Wars tend to breed military mimicries. Successful units soon enough find themselves being countered by similar forces on the other side in the way that newly-developed weapons soon enough are offset by newly-developed defences against them. In South Africa the success of the Boer style of combat led, after rather too long, to the use of mounted infantry and, within that framework and constantly spurred by Boer raiding parties and commandos, to the raising of small and largely irregular units to operate well away from central bases and field headquarters. With that development, with small and nearly-independent commands in fairly isolated areas, the constraints of military discipline could be expected to slacken and sometimes to disappear, the more so when the men employed were drawn largely from among the less rigid ranks of colonial volunteers enlisting often enough for extra pay and the potential for some freedom of violent action and possibly some loot.

2

Crimes

Generally speaking, the men who joined the irregular units were likely to be pretty much of a type. Almost all of them were seasoned in South Africa by then, having served out a period of enlistment and signed on for another period in this newer employment. All of them were, at the least, competent horsemen and weapons managers because, unless they were, they simply would not have lasted in units demanding those qualities for continued existence. They were accustomed to living out and living rough and being able to doctor their animals to some extent. They dressed in a style considerably less parade-worthy than even the more regular colonial units, let alone the punctilious British.

Beyond these similarities they diverged only in some aspects of their natures—some of them were more literate, some more capable of leadership, some were 'gentlemen', some were 'bad hats', some were adventurers, and some had simply gone along to be with their mates. To that extent a unit like the Bush Veldt Carbineers was hardly different from any other regimental mixed-bag. The difference came with the added factors of distance from headquarters, smallness of patrols, difficult terrain, and the fighting ability of the enemy and his willingness to do whatever was necessary in defence of his land. With the anti-Boer irregulars in the field, fire met fire and there erupted a blaze of bitter actions that were small and savage and usually marked by a great indifference towards the accepted rules of war.

The word 'atrocity' has been used so often in the days since the second World War that it has lost some of its hard-edged horror. Certainly men-at-arms throughout history have dealt harshly with their opponents and with civilians but, with the opening of the twentieth century, the normality was (in the popular mind at least)

Above: One of the Bushmen with his horse in the field. *Below:* The Seaforth Highlanders 'marching easy'. Although their kilts offer a blaze of colour to marksmen, by this time their tunics were khaki and their helmets had khaki covers over the white pipeclay (*Photos: Australian War Memorial*)

that soldiers fought one another, observed a code of conduct which was tough but humane, and treated civil populations with some decency. The Boer War changed all that.

The Boer forces were not an army in the understood sense of the word. They were a part of the totality of South Africa's European population with a barely-perceptible dividing line between civilian and soldier; they fought out of uniform and their bases were townships and settlements and farms of their own people—just as their supply lines, communications, and intelligence came from those people. Their most capable generals were not soldiers by training or vocation: Piet Joubert was a successful and wealthy businessman and investor; Piet Cronje was a farmer and Native Commissioner; Louis Botha and Koos De la Rey were farmers, and De la Rey was also a politician; Christiaan De Wet was a businessman and Jan Smuts a lawyer.

With almost no exception the men they led against the British were, like them, drawn from the land and the professions, from trades and crafts and small stores, and they fought to protect and hold their own. That they used methods which were, by British military standards, less than scrupulous is not surprising for they had

Civilian-soldier leaders. General Christiaan De Wet (hands crossed) and his staff (*Photo: Australian War Memorial*)

to fight large and well-drilled forces which were themselves sustained by the whole economic power of the Empire—and by the morale inherent in what Britain had done in the past and what she held in the world of that day.

So, for the Boers, when an opportunity offered to slow that machine, to set it running erratically, they seized on it. If a successful raid could be added to by piling humiliation on the losers so much the better, and the use of British arms and supplies against their previous owners, the stripping of prisoners and sending them back to their lines naked and raw under the sun, the calculated arrogance of dropping troops in the centre of an advancing mass at ranges over a thousand metres (and then disappearing)—all these things were of a setting in which the Boers were anxious to prove how successful they could be. There was always the implication that God and right were on their side.

For the British and the Boer alike there was the need to show their people success and the essential wrongness of the enemy. Propaganda was blatant and coarse and, for much of the time, lacking in anything other than a small seed of truth. On both sides stories were spread and published about brutal actions, about enemy

These Boer pickets posed for their picture early in the war (*Photo: Australian War Memorial*)

Heavily-armoured trains offered a fair degree of protection but were not immune to track-mining and derailment—a favourite Boer manoeuvre (*Photo: Australian War Memorial*)

savagery, about atrocities (and it is certain that there was evidence to show that things were done which were not simply military actions). Looting was widespread. British troops ransacked and pillaged, usually for food and liquor but if there was anything else that caught a soldier's fancy he was unlikely to leave it behind. By the same token, if he found nothing he needed or wanted he was as likely as not to destroy in anger whatever there was. The Boers in their turn descended on British-owned farms and stripped and destroyed them, less wantonly perhaps, more as a calculated act of war but just as effectively.

When raiders began to blow up troop and supply trains, and mined railway lines in places suited for ambush, the British responded first by armouring and arming the trains and then by coupling a wagon ahead of a locomotive and filling it with Boer prisoners and civilians who would suffer first in any track-mining explosion. The use of soft-nosed and explosive bullets by some commandos left such mangled and shattered dead and so few wounded that British troops in a number of cases began cross-cutting their own rounds, or using flat-nosed bullets for their tumbling impact and spreading effect.

Whenever a dubious incident happened the telling and re-telling of it amplified the atrocity value so that tales of Boer women and children being shot down by British soldiers were widespread—just as were stories of soldiers taken prisoner and then coldly executed. There was some truth on both sides for both those things happened, neither on more than isolated occasions but both serving as the basis for rampant propaganda and the consequent increase in bitterness and hatred—and so to the likelihood of yet more savage reprisals.

By the time the Bush Veldt Carbineers had been raised, what level of tolerance there may have been between the enemies had dropped almost to disappearing point. Deneys Reitz in his book *Commando* describes one fierce attack on a British cavalry post in which the Boers, dressed in captured army khaki, killed and wounded seventy-odd troopers for their own loss of seven, of whom only one was killed. Reitz goes on to tell how he and his fellows had re-equipped themselves from the savaged Lancers: 'We had ridden into action that morning at our last gasp and we emerged refitted from head to heel . . . fresh horses, fresh rifles . . . and more ammunition than we could carry away. We were like giants refreshed.'

It is hardly difficult to understand, in the light of the Boer methods, why the counter was a tendency to shoot prisoners when they were captured wearing British khaki. When the Canadian Scouts raised by Major Howard found their commander shot to death after his capture they pledged themselves not to take another prisoner, and in doing that they were not departing very far from formal orders which had been issued by Kitchener and renewed by Colonel, later Field-Marshal, Haig that all Boer prisoners captured wearing British uniform should be shot then and there.

Kitchener's drive across the country, the blockhouse system, the destruction of farmhouses, and the internment of women and children, all on top of the intense national feeling of the Boers and the essential differences between the opponents, together had set the stage for this, the end-game of the war. It had degenerated from a war in which an army fought most of a nation to one in which elements of that army fought elements of that nation in outer areas. Meanwhile politicians and generals on both sides were much engaged in trying to end the whole thing, each to his own country's advantage, neither wishing to appear to have given in.

So, beyond the Base Headquarters and the capitals, outside the major garrison areas, by brigades and regiments, by companies and troops, the British pushed past their blockhouses and barbed wire, dressed now in khaki drab, many more of them now mounted, more sure than they had ever been of the country behind them. And the

Boers, fewer in number, more widely dispersed, short supplied in just about everything, fought on with what seemed an increasing ferocity. Well beyond the formal British forward troops, in rough and demanding country which the Boers saw as their own ground, irregular commands skirmished and raided, living much as did the Boer commandos, fighting in the same hard way, making the same sort of on-the-spot and often-savage decisions, and meting out the roughest kind of justice. And sometimes not dealing in justice at all but in revenge.

Quite early in the war there had been raised a troop of nearly two hundred South African guides, men who spoke native dialects or Afrikaans or both, who knew the country intimately and who dressed as did the Boers, the one difference being the strip of animal skin they wore around their wide-brimmed hats. The skin and their commander's name earned them the title of 'Rimington's Tigers', and their task was principally the gathering of intelligence.

Other local troops were raised, in the Cape and in Natal, as the war thundered on and these small units operated almost always as forward scouts or as guides, almost always under direct British command. When the colonies began sending men from Canada, New Zealand, and Australia they, too, tended to be brigaded with British forces, but their presence and their actions and attitudes combined with the Boers' methods to press home the lesson of their usefulness and, in this closing phase of the war, the path was eased for formations of such men to operate more widely, less restricted by higher headquarters and so in a far less orthodox manner.

That eased path led to the formation of the Bush Veldt Carbineers, a strange conjunction between private enterprise and money, the British military machine, and men looking for something out of the ordinary.

3

Crucified

It really ain't the time nor place
To reel off rhyming diction—
But yet we'll write a final rhyme
While waiting crucifixion

Harry Morant,
written while imprisoned

That civilians were shot by British Imperial troops in South Africa is beyond doubt. That captured or wounded British troops were shot by Boers is equally certain. There were instances in which Boers flew flags of surrender, waited till their enemies were in the open and then dropped the white flags and opened fire; just as there were cases in which soldiers, jumpy in the presence of men in ordinary dress, took no chances and shot them down, since the Boers generally wore no form of uniform.

Stories of outrages and atrocities on both sides were, of course, grist to the mills of the popular press in many countries and there were outbursts in print in Europe and America about 'the vile behaviour' of British troops not dissimilar to those in the British press ten years later about the actions of German soldiers in 'poor little Belgium'. There were reports in the London newspapers that Italian and Austrian military observers with Kitchener's headquarters regarded such stories as 'incredible', and the Chamber of Commerce in Bremen, anxious about trade, deplored the outbursts of Anglophobia in German newspapers.

But the stories *were* printed and widely believed and the denials made by Lord Roberts and others were given no space. In Europe and America the Boers were produced as gallant civilians who had

This studio photograph of Boers shows a wide range of rifles (French, German, Belgian, British), all of which were privately owned (*Photo: Australian War Memorial*)

taken up arms in the defence of their homeland against the brutal and expansionist British Empire. Yet the London *Morning Post* in July of 1901 published a statement by a Boer correspondent saying, 'The writer insists that clemency on the part of the British . . . has been misplaced . . . and he further suggests that anyone taking up arms against England after the date mentioned should be hanged'. The date mentioned was in April 1901 at which time, and following the bringing down of a Treason Bill in the Cape Parliament in the previous year, residents in disaffected areas were warned that 'all acts of rebellion against the King would be dealt with under the old common law, and would be punished by death or imprisonment. This step was rendered necessary owing to the discovery that many Dutch colonists were still assisting the Boers either openly or by secret methods.'

Whatever the newspapers had to say, whatever known orders were issued, whatever the political manoeuvres to end the war—for the men in the field survival was paramount. The good soldier

Railway lines were vital links, but for troops on the move there was little or no comfortable accommodation (*Photo: Australian War Memorial*)

(regular, volunteer, conscript, or guerrilla) is the one who preserves himself in order to destroy the enemy, and in the taut-nerved, itchy-fingered business of fighting a raiding war men tended to forget the rigid rules of military law. The interpretation of that law and the orders which spring from it are always subject to the bloodletting circumstance which surrounds the man at the point of the sword and I doubt that there has ever been a war fought in which the fighting soldier has not broken the rules at some stage.

By the time the BVC was in operation so many rules had been broken that, to its less than 'regulation' soldiers, survival had become a matter of steering clear of trouble when that was possible and taking every advantage offered at other times. Behind them, across the face of Africa down to the Cape Colony, their military masters were turning much of the land into a depopulated waste and cramming women and children into concentration camps. Jan Smuts, then a twenty-eight-year-old commando leader wrote, 'Dams everywhere full of rotting animals; water undrinkable. Veld covered with slaughtered herds of sheep and goats, cattle and horses. The horror passes description . . .' With that sort of precedent the officers and men of the BVC were hardly likely to be gentle in their approach to their war.

North and a little east of Pretoria in the Transvaal, and close to 300 kilometres distant, lay the town of Pietersburg, the two linked by a railway line. That double sliver of steel, essential for the movement of men and munitions, ran through country ideal for rough-riding operations—an area known as the Spelonken. It was rugged and rising land, broken and harsh above the veldt, and open to extremes of weather. Scattered across it were the isolated farms which were natural staging points for the Boer commandos riding through; lean and fierce men and formidable fighters in the natural camouflage of their working dress. From the farmers they were able to get shelter and provisions and information about troop and train movements, just as they were able to hide caches of weapons and ammunition in the roofs and cellars of farm buildings, and ride down to the towns and settlements to observe the British army for themselves.

The railway-line was under constant attack from these commandos and, early in 1901, it was decided to raise a corps of 500 men to patrol the area, to protect the line, and to keep the commandos on the run as far as possible. It is difficult to pin down precisely how the unit was brought into being but it seems that while the formality of it came from the Army's Intelligence Department, the impetus came from local businessmen.

Given that the long grind of the war seemed to be slowing and that the massive bulk of the British forces seemed to be in control in the towns, it can be understood that the business and professional people in the wide sweep around Pretoria and Pietersburg should want to be seen to be on the side of the garrisoning troops. For them, and for the inlying growers and traders, the supplying of the soldiers was a matter of maintaining their business life; the marauding attacks of the Boers affected their balance-sheets and their security. Lord Milner, the Governor, wrote to Kitchener saying: 'What the bulk of the people require is protection not punishment. I do not mean to say

Away from the few roads and railway lines there was always a problem of moving supplies and ammunition forward, when it became a matter of brute strength of men and animals (*Photo: Australian War Memorial*)

that they do not all hate us. They do. But they love their property more than they hate the British and would be glad to see the back of the guerillas.'

It is known that a storekeeper named Levy from Pienaar's River along the railway-line put up £500 towards a mounted corps to operate in his area of the Spelonken. At Matapan, a little further out, a Dr Neel contributed £100 and the same amount came in from Mr Kelly, a Pretoria merchant. They were joined by a number of smaller contributors and their interest and money prompted the Intelligence Department to sponsor the raising of a corps to be known as the Bush Veldt Carbineers—the BVC. Despite that initial monetary impetus the corps was not a body of mercenaries in the accepted sense; it was an official Imperial military unit, equipped, armed, uniformed, and paid by the Army, even if the standard of dress was hardly uniform, even if they had no unit badge.

Recruiting for the BVC was widespread and attracted a predominance of colonial volunteers, largely Australians, men whose enlistments were time-expired or getting close to it, and it is certain that Kitchener approved the scheme, recognising as he did the need for more mounted infantry and recognising, too, that the colonials were excellent material for the kind of war he was now fighting.

The planned number of 500 was never reached. The BVC eventually mustered close to 350 all ranks and among them Harry Morant's name appeared in the January to March volume of the British Army List for 1901 as a lieutenant. The roll of officers included the three men who had begun the whole thing and who followed their funds into the unit: Levy as Captain/Paymaster, Neel as the Medical Officer, and Kelly as a lieutenant. British officers joining were Lieutenants Picton, Midgelly, and Bright, with Captain Hunt coming in a little later. The Australians were Captain Mortimer, who was Quartermaster for a short while, and Lieutenants Hannam, Edwards, Baudinet, Handcock (the Veterinary and Transport Officer), and Witton, who had enlisted thirty men and brought them along as artillery teams although the guns never materialised. The men were a similar mix of Australians, British, and South Africans and the unit was commanded by Major Robert Lenehan, another Australian.

If they had a single common characteristic it was that their capacity for either giving or taking orders was doubtful, even if their belligerency and dislike for formal discipline was certain. With the entry of the Bush Veldt Carbineers on to the stage of the Spelonken the first act of a tragedy began. Yet the six men who were to be most affected by that impending tragedy were not savages, not deliberate

Some Boer farmhouses, like this one, were not very gracious but were as strongly built as many British blockhouses and were sometimes used as such (*Photo: Australian War Memorial*)

or wanton killers: two more-or-less-professional soldiers (one British, one Australian), two lawyers, a blacksmith, and a bushman-balladeer—as much of a cross-section as any small group of men drawn from an army may be. That they were together in that place, at that time, and in those circumstances was a matter of chance—chance reinforced by inclination and, for four of them at least, perhaps some shared weakness in their natures.

HARRY PICTON

Here is the most shadowy figure among the six, a man of whom little is known either before or after those climactic days in South Africa. The Picton name has shown up in Britain's military history for generations. There was a Sir Grenville, an adventurer who rode off to do battle with the Turks; John Picton was a general in India; and Sir Thomas commanded Wellington's 5th Division at Waterloo. But the family is widespread and fragmented and, because of some of its lusty ancestors, the stock includes numbers of illegitimate offspring. There has been a long tradition of passing on the family name through legitimate daughters so that as well as a strain in the West Indies there are hyphenated versions of it in south Wales and in Western Australia.

If Harry Picton fits into that ancient military line at all, though, it's probably at some remove. On his enrolment papers he listed his next-of-kin as his father—'Alfred Picton, of 55, Abbacore Crescent, Lewisham, Kent' and he gave his own occupation at enlistment as 'Horsebreaker'. He joined Loch's Horse, one of those essentially British and almost-private regiments, raised in January 1900 by a committee headed initially by Lord Loch and numbering among its officers a retired Lieutenant-Colonel serving as a troop captain with a lieutenant in his troop who was a retired Royal Navy commander! Picton served well with the unit in South Africa, was promoted to Corporal in 'B' Troop, and performed gallantly on two recognised occasions.

This account is taken from the history of Loch's Horse. 'An instance of extraordinary courage by a trooper . . . has been brought to the special notice of General Hunter today. A troop of Loch's Horse were recently out on patrol . . . and somehow they rode into an ambush. Lieutenant Williams was almost immediately killed and Colonel Ross dangerously wounded in the head. At this critical juncture Trooper Picton gallantly rushed up to the wall . . . from which the enemy had opened their unexpected fire, and discovered six Boers still there. He immediately emptied his revolver with such effect that three of the Boers fell dead, and the remainder forthwith laid down their arms and were taken prisoners. Trooper Picton for his gallant action has been recommended for the medal for distinguished service in the field.'

He had enlisted in March 1900 and by the time he ended his service with Loch's Horse fourteen months later he had spent a couple of months attached to the Intelligence staff and had been promoted to sergeant, as well as being again recommended for his behaviour in the bloody fight at Bothaville. There, for several hours, artillery on both sides engaged at close range and Boers and mounted infantry fought hand-to-hand, each side within immediate range of shells and sniper-fire. The bloodletting ended with the bayonet and, in view of what was to happen later, it is revealing to find that the British troops were so enraged at some of the Boers using explosive, soft-nosed bullets that prisoners found with them in their pockets were at once ordered to be shot. The execution was only stopped by the intervention of the commanding general.

There are letters of recommendation, produced by Picton in court later, which give some idea of his merit as a soldier. One of his commanders wrote: 'Sergeant Picton came out with Loch's Horse . . . in February, 1901. He has given entire satisfaction to his officers, and I am very pleased to state I have found him not only very plucky in action, but steady and painstaking in the execution of his duty. He has been recommended for the D.S.M. Having been under my personal command for some time, I cannot speak too highly of his conduct.'

His regimental commander's letter said: 'This is to introduce to you Sergeant Picton of my corps, Loch's Horse. He is a worthy fellow and well connected, and is seeking a commission. Could you help him in getting such in your regiment? I understand you have some vacancies.' It seems likely that that letter was addressed to Major Lenehan when he was engaged in recruiting for the Bush Veldt Carbineers, and the mention of Picton's being 'well connected' may argue some link, however distant, with the old family.

That Harry Picton should have been twice commended for his actions in the field and recommended by his officers for efficiency, steadiness, and worthiness hardly argues that he was naturally a rash, temperamental, or bloodthirsty man. That he was adventurous is sure—there is a strong suggestion that he had served in the French Foreign Legion before the Boer War—and that he intended to follow an army career seems possible on his CO's statement that he was 'seeking a commission'. Given that he could achieve officer status quickly with the BVC, and probably see some extra action, his presence with that unit in the Spelonken is understandable. Of the men arrested and tried he appears to have had the least to say and the least said about him. But he was there and linked with Harry Morant from the day their names appeared together in the first volume of the 1901 Army List . . . 'Sgt. H. G. Picton as Lieutenant to Bush Veldt Carbineers'.

GEORGE RAMSDALE WITTON

As the century turned George Witton was a gunner in the Victorian Permanent Artillery, stationed at Fort Franklin in Victoria. From a farming family, Witton had broken away from the land and enlisted for a five-year term of service in the Colony's forces having already spent two years with a Volunteer Corps, the Victorian Rangers. He was a tall young man —188 centimetres—and well set up, used to horses and an outdoor life and, very likely, ideal material for a soldier. He was fit, strong, keen, and seemingly of a quiet nature, well-mannered, and considerate. Several men who served with him when he was a ranker and some under his later command remarked on his 'humanity'; Sergeant-Major Hammett, of the Bush Veldt Carbineers, in an affidavit wrote that he found Witton 'to be a thorough officer and a gentleman . . . (who) carried out to the strict letter of the law the orders he received from his superior officer only.' The man hardly sounds like any sort of roistering killer.

With the outbreak of the war Witton and his fellow gunners expected to be sent to South Africa, but the days and weeks dragged away with no sign of their going and contingent after contingent was formed and sent off while they waited. Tiring of the delay, and impatient to see some action, he asked for an exchange into the fourth contingent to be raised in Victoria, the Imperial Bushmen. He wrote of his feelings at that time in the florid prose which perhaps best sums up the old Empire attitude: 'I could not rest content until I had offered the assistance one man could give to our beloved Queen and the great nation to which I belong.' The new regiment called for just the sort of man Witton was—he'd been born in the bush, could ride almost as soon as he could walk, and had learned to shoot from infancy. All that plus his Volunteer Corps experience and a year

Colonel Robert Baden-Powell at the age of 43. Famous as the founder of the Boy Scout movement 'B-P' sprang to fame for his defence of Mafeking during the Boer War, for which he was promoted to Major-General (*Photo: Australian War Memorial*)

served with the Artillery made him a certainty and he sailed with the regiment and its 700 horses on 1 May 1900, a newly-promoted corporal.

The contingent landed not at Cape Town but at Beira, on the east coast of Africa, and there they spent their time exercising their horses, drilling, and waiting to go south to Durban or west into the Transvaal. Mafeking had been relieved, the battle fought at Eland's River, and troops passed through with tales of hard fighting and excitements; the only break in the monotony for George Witton was that he went down with a severe case of synovitis in his right knee. The joint was so badly swollen that he could neither ride nor march and he spent two weeks in hospital where he was told he would be sent home to Australia. In answer to his pleading not to be returned home he was then sent on the long and slow journey down to Durban and on to Cape Town where he was posted to the Australian Depot at Maitland, eight kilometres outside the city. There, although still lame, he assisted the Quartermaster-Sergeant.

It was three months after that that he met an Australian officer who told him he was raising a corps of irregulars and could arrange to get him into it if he could muster a gun-section to join it. Witton wasted no time in recruiting thirty-odd men—a few Imperial Royal Horse Artillerymen and the rest time-expired Australians. He applied for and got his discharge from his own regiment, was advised that he had been given a commission in the irregular unit, and reached Pietersburg on 13 July 1901, almost fourteen months after sailing from Victoria. The Australian officer who had told him about the unit was its commander, Major Robert Lenehan; the unit was the Bush Veldt Carbineers.

On that mid-July day Lieutenant Witton was twenty-seven years old. He had served as a volunteer in three regiments before joining the BVC, had spent more than a year of the Boer War in Africa, had never commanded men in the field, and had not seen a single day's fighting. By the time he was twenty-eight he would be a life-sentence prisoner.

This posed picture of some Boers was taken during their four-month-long siege of Ladysmith (*Photo: Australian War Memorial*)

ROBERT WILLIAM LENEHAN

The Lenehan family of New South Wales was, in the nineteenth century, industrious, wealthy, and with some considerable influence in Catholic circles. They owned property in several parts of Sydney, as well as a prosperous cabinet-making business, and they were generous in their support of the Church, giving land and buildings for the use of monastic orders.

Robert William, a student at both Riverview and St Ignatius colleges, was well brought up and, in the Sydney of those times at the end of the century, could fairly be considered a child of some privilege. He was good enough at his books to move on to the study of law at the University of Sydney and there to find an interest in the volunteer military forces — an interest likely to have been as much social as martial for many young men. For Lenehan, though, it seems to have been something more for it persisted through most of his life.

At the outbreak of the Boer War he was a reasonably successful lawyer with offices in the central part of the city of Sydney, and he was a Major in the New South Wales Volunteer Artillery. By that time he had served under the command of Major-General Edward Hutton, an old Etonian who had been stationed in New South Wales from 1893 to 1896, who had then gone to Canada to re-organise the militia force there, and who became a field commander in South Africa.

Lenehan took a drop in rank in order to get away to the Boer War. He was attached to the second contingent of the New South Wales Mounted Rifles as a Captain commanding B Squadron, and sailed for Cape Town on 17 January 1900. During Lord Roberts' advance from Paardeburg to Pretoria Lenehan held command of his squadron and, it seems, took over some other troops of Mounted Rifles as well to expand his command to the size of a wing of scouting and flanking horse. His Queen's South Africa Medal, in the possession of his youngest son Roger, shows six clasps for his participation in the actions of 1900 and 1901 and there is nothing to show he was anything but a competent commander.

He was a burly man, heavily moustached in the fashion of the times, and with a splendid seat on a horse; indeed, he was recognised as a fine rider and it was at pre-war race meetings, and the social events which followed them, that he had first made the acquaintance of Harry Morant and the two had hit it off well enough — both with a deep love for horses, both hard men. But whether it was part of the more free-wheeling Australian character, or whether Lenehan had exhibited some trait or performed some deed which went against the old Etonian grain, General Hutton seems to have not liked him. Writing in 1903 Hutton said he had 'the very poorest opinion' of Lenehan, although he made no attempt to explain why.

It has been impossible to discover what led Captain Lenehan to apply for a posting to the just-raised Bush Veldt Carbineers. Perhaps it was a liking for the military life which had long attracted him; perhaps the prospect of advancement; perhaps the freedom of action which may well have been more appealing to him than the constrictions of a legal office in Sydney. The fact that he knew he was on the wrong side of General Hutton and wanted to get away from his sphere of command, without going back to Australia, may well have had something to do with it. Whatever the motive he requested the posting, the New South Wales Government was asked to extend his leave and allow him to be used (remember, he was officially still on the strength of the NSW Artillery), and he found himself promoted to Major and placed in command of the BVC.

His headquarters was at Pietersburg and there, generally speaking, he stayed, effectively no more than the administrative head of a unit which rapidly became involved in anything but administrative tasks. He was to be promoted again and to hold command again—but never in action or outside Australia.

Major Robert Lenehan taken after his return from the Boer War (*Photo: Courtesy of Lenehan family*)

Private A. Du Frayer, NSW Mounted Rifles, in Dress uniform; the sash is the 'Queen's Scarf', a special award for bravery, crocheted by Queen Victoria and now in the Australian War Memorial (*Photo: Australian War Memorial*)

Major Robert Lenehan, a superb horseman, mounted on a favourite horse (*Photo: Courtesy of Lenehan family*)

JAMES FRANCIS THOMAS

'Regimental Order No. 13, N.S.W. Mounted Infantry HQ, Sydney, 13–2–1891.
The following extract from General Order No. 22, 10–2–1891.
His Excellency the Governor with the advice of the Executive Council has been pleased to make the following appointment in the Volunteer Force. Mr. James Francis Thomas to be 2nd. Lieutenant in the Tenterfield Company, Mounted Infantry Regiment.'

He was thirty years old, the son of a farmer from the western side of Sydney, and a graduate in law from the University of Sydney. He was a tall, rather thin man with a good seat on a horse and a good head for business. In the year in which his commission was gazetted he was reasonably well established as a solicitor in Tenterfield, up in the far north of New South Wales, close to the Queensland border. It was then, as it is now, lush country, well watered, well timbered, and with the sort of independence which has long made the people up there call the area 'New England'. In Tenterfield the sort of law that needed practising was pretty straightforward: wills, conveyancing, bills of sale—nothing dramatic or outstanding. The pressure was light enough to allow a young and unattached lawyer to socialise and to indulge himself in a respectable hobby; and Thomas was able to combine both by joining the Volunteers.

Even by the time he first put on its uniform that local unit had a budding tradition. In 1885 an Independent Unit was formed calling itself the Upper Clarence Light Horse, with a detachment in Tenterfield. Three years afterwards the NSW Mounted Infantry Regiment was formed and the Tenterfield lads became half of A Company. In 1894, six years after the first unit was raised and three years after his commissioning, Thomas passed out of the Second Cavalry School of Instruction, was promoted to First Lieutenant and took over command of the Tenterfield Half-Company from Captain C. H. E. Chauvel, the man who had originally raised the Upper Clarence Light Horse. In May 1895 Thomas was promoted to Captain and drew praise from the Major-General Commanding who wrote, after the Annual Inspection: 'A very high standard of Efficiency has been reached by the Tenterfield Half Company and an excellent Military Spirit . . . exists.'

Thomas was obviously a good soldier and a good leader, as well as being a very capable country solicitor and a man interested and active

The Tenterfield Mounted Rifles sprang from the Upper Clarence Light Horse. This officer in the unit's Parade Dress is Lieutenant Harry Chauvel, later Major-General Sir Harry (*Photo: Australian War Memorial*)

in politics. It was a stirring time in the Australian Colonies then, as the century circled towards its close. Federation of the Colonies had been advocated for more than ten years with a former Premier of New South Wales, Sir Henry Parkes, spearheading the movement. Thomas was deeply interested in this piece of practical politics and he sank his capital into the purchase of a newspaper, the *Tenterfield Star*, so that he could support the cause. Indeed, he was one of the men most concerned with persuading Parkes to stop over at Tenterfield on his way back from Queensland to Sydney, and it was in a hall there that Sir Henry delivered a major and telling speech in favour of Federation.

By the outbreak of the Boer War, then, James Francis Thomas was thirty-eight, a successful lawyer, a newspaper proprietor, a considerable figure in the local social and political life, and commander of the district's Volunteer Forces. It was no surprise that he was asked to raise a contingent for active service in South Africa and he volunteered at once, although he didn't go with that first contingent in November 1899. He left for the Cape three months later, and the General Order of 28 February 1900 lists him as the Officer Commanding A Squadron of the NSW Bushmen's Contingent which sailed that day.

Thomas clearly kept on being a good soldier during the fighting in South Africa; commanding in the field as he had at home, earning his campaign clasps, never spectacular, always efficient. He was promoted to Major and, but for the events in that courtroom, he almost certainly would have gone back to New England and his two hats—the lawyer's and the newspaperman's.

It has not been possible to find out why Thomas was selected as Defending Officer. Certainly there were other men of law in the Australian forces in South Africa; equally surely there were some among them with more relevant experience than a country solicitor with no trial background worth mentioning. None of the accused men had ever heard of this mounted infantry major and, indeed, Morant had put in his own bid for a defence counsel—and a pretty impertinent bid at that. There is a minute sheet of January 1902 the subject of which is 'Trial of Lieut. Morant'. It goes on, 'Request to know if Capt. Purland will be available and willing to defend above.'

Over the signature of the Assistant Secretary to the Transvaal Administration the next entry says: 'The Director of Prisons. For your report, please. Should you be agreeable to act as desired, the formal (?) of this Administration would be needed, under such unusual circumstances.'

The reply from the Director of Prisons made no bones about his feelings. 'I am astonished that Lieut. Morant should have made such a request. I have only the slightest acquaintance with him and he should be aware that my official position prevents my undertaking such a duty as he suggests—even if I had the inclination.' It is signed by the indignant Captain Purland.

It is difficult to know if Morant was being brash or engaging in some bold humour, although that seems unlikely under the circumstances. The logical thing is to assume that he knew little about correct procedures and had, perhaps, been struck with the authority of the Director of Prisons. However, Morant and the others found Thomas in their corner—and a late arrival at that.

Witton says that it was Lenehan who engaged Thomas for his own defence, and it is more than likely that the two had some passing acquaintance within the legal fraternity. In any case the whole of Thomas's first day on the scene was taken up with interviewing Lenehan. It was not until the following day that Thomas was able to spend short periods of time with the others and, although he was entered into the court as counsel for the prisoners, the whole affair had then to be adjourned in order for Headquarters to be signalled seeking authority for him to take on the defence brief.

To that time, as he neared his fortieth birthday, James Francis Thomas had every reason to consider his life as being tolerably successful. He had gone from a farm boy to established positions in country society, in backroom politics, in the press, and in the military. Now, although he had no way of knowing it, he was to gain a strange sort of eminence, almost of notoriety, and to move his life into ways he could never have suspected and would not have desired.

PETER JOSEPH HANDCOCK

Bathurst lies about 200 kilometres west of Sydney, across the Blue Mountains and on the edge of the great sweep of the western plains. It is a large and thriving country town nowadays and even in the closing third of the nineteenth century it was a place of some importance, a major staging-point for travellers to and from the coast, and a focus for the farming and mining of a wide district. Blacksmithing was one of the vital trades there at that time and it was to a smithy that the young Peter Joseph Handcock was sent to learn a craft. He was twelve then, a country boy, born a few kilometres from Bathurst at Peel, brought up in the bush, sturdy, and obedient.

The ten years which followed saw him grow into the sort of man the anvil makes — tall, not bulky but solid and very strong, good at his work, good with horses, and looked on as 'steady'. In later years a Bathurst resident wrote this description of him: 'He was a fine type of the silent Australian, essentially a doer, not a talker. Resourceful and a grafter he was never out of work. Morally and physically clean-living, careful financially, he was no rude overstepper of social conventions.'

This ideal-sounding fellow was obviously a pretty good catch and he was married at twenty-one. By the turn of the century he was a little past thirty, settled in his life, it seemed, with three children (the oldest a boy of ten), and a reasonable job as a blacksmith with the Railways Department. Yet there was obviously something more to him than the sort of quiet rectitude implied in the words of that Bathurst resident, something less placid. Perhaps it was a drive for a better life or for excitement, the feeling that he was simply being

Left: Trooper Peter Handcock, Shoeing-smith, in a studio portrait taken in Sydney just before his contingent sailed for The Cape. *Below:* Two short scribblings written by Peter Handcock while awaiting his execution (*Photos: Author's collection*)

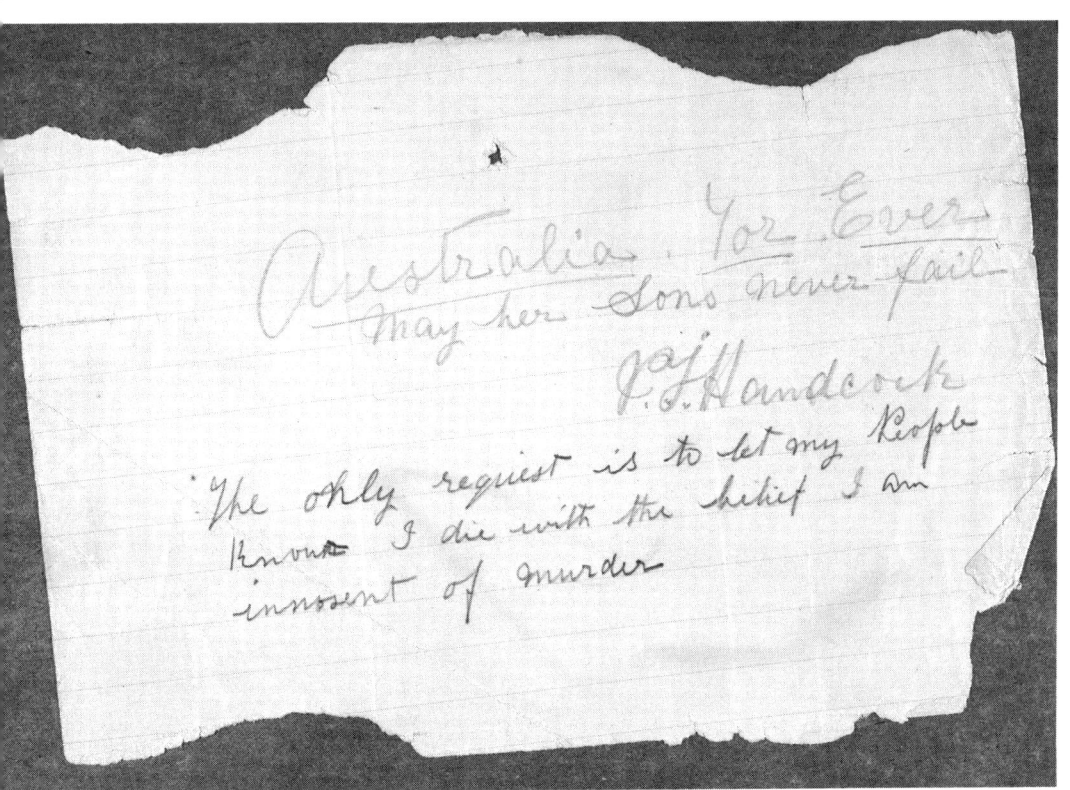

"Australia For Ever
May her Sons never fail
P.J. Handcock

The only request is to let my People know I die with the belief I am innocent of murder"

carried along with no hand in his own destiny. Whatever it may have been, when the second contingent of troops was being raised to go to South Africa, Peter Handcock was working in the bush at Manildra and he told his workmates there that he wanted to 'go for a soldier' and asked them not to say a word of it to his family.

He went down to Sydney on his Railways pass, offered himself for enlistment, passed the medical, and was enrolled as No. 488 in C Company, 2nd New South Wales Mounted Infantry, with the classification of Shoeing-Smith. Then he went home and told his wife and family of his twelve-month enlistment and, almost before they were used to the idea, he was gone. The contingent sailed for the Cape on 17 January 1900 and Handcock was never to see Australia again.

Although there is nothing outstanding in his record during that year of service he was plainly a good soldier-tradesman for he was promoted to Farrier-Sergeant and then, when the men of his contingent were preparing to sail home again, he elected to stay behind. Under that quiet, almost-stolid exterior, Peter Handcock seems to have hidden some fire, some ambition.

This souvenir sent home by Peter Handcock was embroidered on a piece of khaki shirt. The original is in the Bathurst Museum

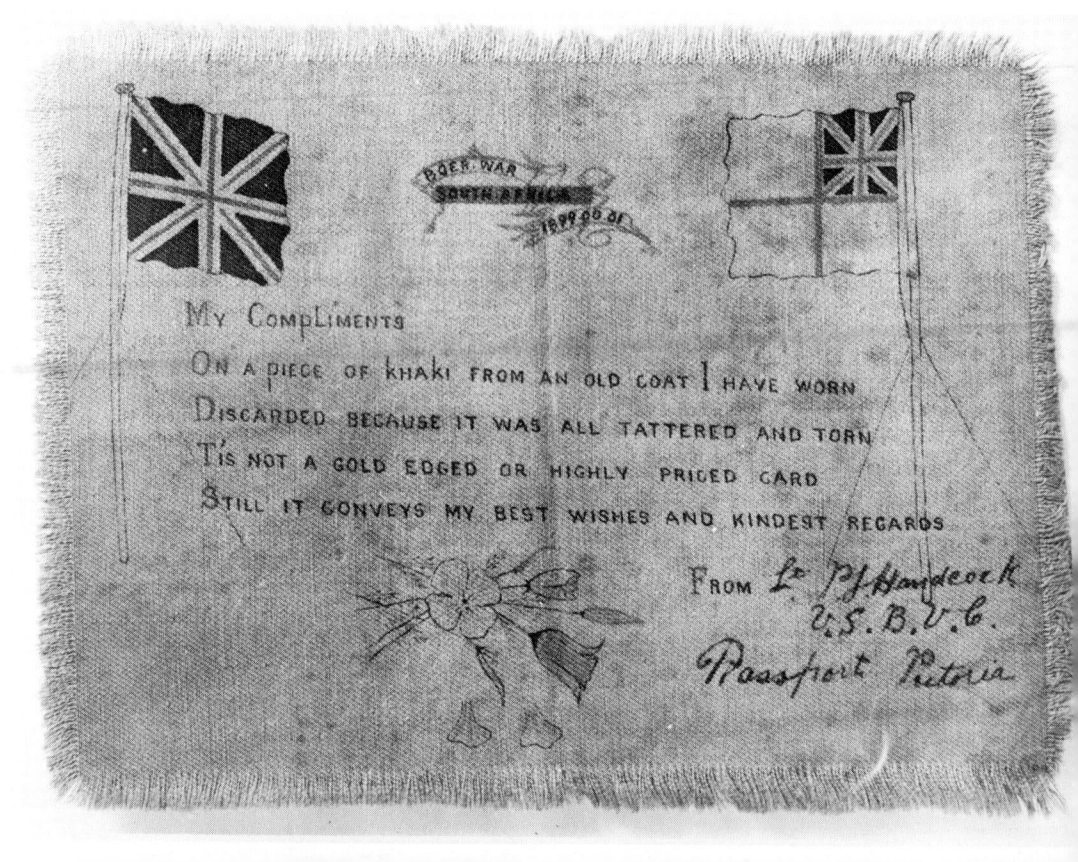

This sergeant of the Camden Troop, NSW Mounted Rifles, is immaculate in Parade Dress (*Photo: Australian War Memorial*)

He wrote to his wife saying that it was no use to return to New South Wales because there was so little work there and he told her that, anyway, he loved a soldier's life and had got a further promotion. With two other sergeants he was commissioned as a Lieutenant in the Bush Veldt Carbineers, where he appeared on the rolls as Veterinary and Transport Officer. Men with whom he had served his enlistment year gave their opinions of him to the press later. One said: 'He was with us as shoeing-smith and a more courteous and obliging fellow you could not meet. Every soldier who knew him respected him. During the whole time he was with our contingent his conduct was excellent and he never gave any idea that he would do anything brutal.'

The Adjutant of the 2nd New South Wales Mounted Rifles wrote of him, and his new unit: 'I was sorry he remained behind to join the Bush Veldt Carbineers. They are composed of a mixed lot, the pickings of the men of every corps who were left behind. In fact I might add that many of the men forming the BVC had been charged when in other contingents with shooting surrendered Boers, had been court-martialled and got off.' The Adjutant spoke of Handcock as a really good man, the best of them, and he expressed regret at seeing him with a regiment which, he said, was so discredited in South Africa.

It seems strange that a man so universally liked, even admired, should have ended his life as he did, facing a firing-squad. There is no record of any word being spoken against him in his civilian life and nothing adverse in his time as a soldier—until after his arrest. That Bathurst resident wrote in April 1902: 'He was a devoted friend, a fair but bitter enemy. If half the charges urged against him are true, then war must have fostered a blood lust and boodle lust that were absent from his actions in this country. That he ever initiated an outrage I must doubt, but that, carried away by the arguments of another (he was too silent to argue) he may have countenanced, or even assisted, is possible. If he did so Peter Handcock would face death with pleasure rather than go back on that mate, even though he left a wife and three loved children to mourn him.'

George Witton, who served with him and was tried alongside him, said that he was never a bloodthirsty desperado, only the chosen tool of unprincipled men; that he had a keen sense of duty and could be relied on to fulfil it and that there was never a braver man.

The admirable and unexceptionable Peter Joseph Handcock was to be tried on five charges of murder and received two sentences of death. By then, of course, he had been closely associated for some months with Harry Morant.

HARRY HARBORD MORANT—'The Breaker'

Here was a man whose life and death held all the ingredients of romantic fiction. The self-proclaimed son of an old and honourable house, a hard-fisted bushman, a versifier, womaniser, drunkard, gambler, a brilliant horseman, social success, brave soldier, and a ruthless adversary who was near-heroic in the manner of his death. It is all there in the legend which has built around him—and some of it is true.

It has been suggested that he was, in fact, not Harry Harbord Morant but Edwin Henry Murrant, son of a workhouse-keeper and his wife, that he was married in Queensland, a welsher on his marriage as he had welshed on a number of bets and debts. Certainly there is an amount of circumstantial material which goes some way towards establishing his birth and name along those lines, provided that the initial premiss is correct, and that it is taken as fact that the papers which support the theory do, in truth, refer to the man who became known as The Breaker.

But there are one or two things which still leave fair room for doubt. Morant always claimed that he was the son of Admiral Sir George Digby Morant but the London press carried a short paragraph on 4 April 1902 which said: 'Admiral Sir George Morant has denied the statement that Lieut. Morant was his son. He declares that the deceased officer was in no way related to him.' That is straightforward enough and entirely understandable, whether the Admiral was concerned to make the record truthful or just as concerned to keep the family name and his own career safe from smears and innuendos.

Morant is an old and proud name in England, especially in the south and west and the research carried out by Carnegie and Shields for their book *In Search of Breaker Morant* certainly shows that the workhouse-keeping Murrants were, at one stage, working at Honiton, in Devonshire—and Harry Morant always claimed that he was a Devon man. But the Head of Record Services in the County of Devon says in a letter: 'We have searched the Bideford Anglican parish registers of baptisms from June 1865 to the end of 1867 but can find no record of the baptism of Henry Harbord Morant.'

Neither the Devon nor the Somerset county archivist, in a general search, found evidence of a birth registered in that name and the British Registrar of Births and Deaths had no listing whatever of *any* male Morant being born across that period. Admiral Sir George was married in 1866—a touch late for The Breaker, who claimed to have been born in the year before that and who may well have been born then, but not to the Admiral's wife (or not legitimately). And as far as parish registers go there is always the possibility that he was never entered into the Anglican church, or any other for that matter.

Where did the 'Harbord' he used as his middle name come from? There was a Horatio Harbord Morant in the late 1800s who was ADC to Queen Victoria, but it was hardly a common name and for an impostor to have chosen it would surely mean either a considerable coincidence or some fairly close knowledge of the family.

Charles Ansell Morant was a cousin of the Hampshire–Devonshire branches of the family, although he was born in India, settled in Renmark, South Australia, became a prominent fruit-grower there, and died in Adelaide in 1966. His long-time friend

Charles Ansell Morant

Miss Hilda Truman of Adelaide has told me in letters and in conversation that Charles always considered Harry to be his relative; as did the Cutlack family of South Australia, a household where The Breaker was a frequent visitor, a friend of the father of the house, and known well enough for F. M. Cutlack to have detailed in his book *Breaker Morant* much of what that family knew of Harry's life, although it must be understood that those details were supplied by Harry and with no supporting proof.

Both Charles Ansell and his father, Lieutenant-Colonel Charles

May Allen Morant, wrote to England seeking recognition of Harry but, according to Miss Truman, the only reply they received was a plain 'No comment', which can be construed as you wish. Yet, if you look at the one surviving photograph of Charles Ansell Morant, and compare it with those of Harry, there is a very strong facial resemblance.

Miss Truman, in a letter, recalls, 'A mystery surrounds his banishment from England—there was a suggestion of scandal in high places . . . card debts . . . Navy!', but the Navy List across that period shows no listing for a Harry or Henry Harbord Morant. It has been suggested to me that the Naval reference may well have been to an older member of the family and that the 'scandal in high places' could refer to an affair between him and another woman, possibly a servant. It is even possible to consider some sort of liaison between one of the Morant women and a local man or an estate servant, and either of those things would have been enough to ensure that the matter was kept well hushed-up.

It seems unlikely that we shall ever know for sure whether Morant was what he claimed, or the son of Murrant the workhouse-master, or something in-between; but there are those one or two unanswered questions which make me feel he was more than simply the Murrant boy. His correspondence and his verses show a command of the language which surely, in those days, must have argued a fair standard of education and a grounding well above the three Rs. His acceptance in Society—even the rather provincial society of Australia in the late 1800s—argues that he could carry himself properly and be accepted at polite dinner-tables and in exclusive clubs. Either he was (in the understood sense of the word) a gentleman, or the man was a consummate actor—which is, of course, entirely possible.

What is undoubted is his horsemanship. There are stories and witnesses enough to his skill and courage in the saddle as a racer, a hurdler, and a polo-player and, in the mordant but realistic humour of the Australian bush, no man could have earned the reputation of The Breaker without good cause. An article by the Australian writer Frank Clune begins, 'Harry Morant was one of the most reckless riders who ever threw leg across wild horse in Australia—and that is a big claim'.

The Scots poet Will Ogilvie spent twelve years in Australia and lived as a drover and stationhand and horsebreaker, much as Morant did. The two met at Nelanguloo Station in Queensland and there was an immediate friendship, especially when they found a common delight in rhyming. Ogilvie recalled in later years a time when

Morant took a bet at the bar of the Exchange Hotel in Parkes that he could put his horse Cavalier over a two-metre paling fence. He mounted the horse at midnight and, by the light of kerosene lamps and flickering candles, backed the ten metres available in the hotel's yard and lifted Cavalier clear of the fence and into the narrow lane beyond.

It didn't always work that well. In the *Nepean Times* of 4 December 1897, on the 'Local and General' page under the heading 'Accidents', there appeared the following: 'On Saturday afternoon Mr. Harry Morant ("The Breaker") mounted a brown mare belonging to Mr. Tom Dobson in the *Nepean Times* yard. The animal reared right over on top of "The Breaker" who was at once taken inside and attended to by Dr. Barber. On Friday he got out again and, though somewhat weak, is pretty right.'

One old-timer in Orange told me that he could remember the day that Morant drove a mob of cattle through the town at five o'clock one morning. The local paper later reported, 'The Breaker was in his highest element of glee as, yelling wildly and loudly, he urged the mob to greater efforts. Morant had been enjoying a drinking bout and, it is surmised, and probably correctly, that he had undertaken the above mentioned "job" to decide some healthy bets.'

In another western New South Wales town, Walgett, it was reported that 'the way Morant would kill wild savage boars with a knife caused many a brave man to almost shudder and gasp with incredulousness. It appeared that Morant did not know the meaning of fear.'

No matter what his origins were in Britain, in Australia he was known from Queensland, south through the country towns of Orange and Parkes and Gulgong, south again into the Nepean and Hawkesbury River country, across New South Wales, through Victoria, and into the riverland of South Australia—known for his riding and horse-breaking skills, for some monumental drunken bouts, and his willingness to gamble, particularly on his horsemanship, occasionally with his fists. He was known to some publicans and policemen, too, as a man who might ride out without paying a bill or who could be picked up and locked away overnight on a Drunk and Disorderly charge.

It was the publication of his verses in the *Bulletin* of Sydney which carried his reputation across the country, rhymes much in the tradition of the bush-balladists who were popular at the time, and which carried echoes of romantics like Herrick and Christina Rosetti and Byron, a book of whose poems Morant was said to carry with him at all times. Some of his poems show a gentleness and wistfulness

The Breaker's much-loved horse Cavalier was painted in 1896 by Frank Prout Mahony, a Melbourne-born Outback painter who also worked for the *Bulletin* (*Photo: Author's collection*)

which seem alien to the man at large and to contradict his reputation as a womaniser. And there are others, rollicking verses with a wild swing to them and some which have a little of the Kipling feel about them. In one he wrote,

> *Sweethearting's vanity—best to stick*
> *To good tobacco and decent grog,*

which has a good deal of the ring of Kipling's

> *And a woman is only a woman,*
> *But a good cigar is a smoke.*

The *Bulletin* published about sixty of Morant's verses, always under the pen-name 'The Breaker', and there were some others which appeared in country newspapers and more again which were scribbled on bits of paper in pubs in payment for a few drinks or just for the fun of it. Most, if not all, have been long lost, but there were two that were run in the same *Nepean Times* which published that accident notice in 1897, and I believe this is the first time they have been printed since then.

A BALLAD OF BIDGEEBEL.
(And The Guileless Queenslander.)

What time when mus'tring days were done,
    And horses earned a 'spell,'—
Three men from Goorybibil Run
    Rode into Bidgeebel.

Mick Greenhide on a chestnut rode,
    Long Jack on 'Kangaroo,'
And little 'Brumby Bill' 'bestrode
    The white mare 'Cockatoo.'

A 'Crusoe' colt he'd broke and trained,
    Mick Greenhide led beside,
And 'Brumby Bill' had been retained
    This 'Crusoe' colt to ride.

Now this same colt they tried one day
    With Campbell's mare—he raced
At even weights right clean away,
    And from the start outpaced

The old brown mare, whose 'form' they knew,
   So, bar ill-luck befell,
Mick Greenhide thought the colt would do
   To win at Bidgeebel.

'Twas Xmas time in Bidgeebel,
   And station men flocked in,
And many camped at Mac's hotel
   And many camped with Flynn.

A man in moles and cabbage-tree
   Was staying there in town;
'Twas said he had but recently
   From out the Gulf come down.

He said that he'd for Xmas stay;
   And, for a joke, this chap
Entered his old flea-bitten gray
   For the Bidgee Handicap.

Now some of whisky took their fill,
   And some got 'full' on brandy,
But Mick and Jack and Brumby Bill
   Swore they'd 'keep straight' on shandy.

Then loud and furious waxed the noise—
   Each backed some favorite horse,
And all the Goorybibil boys
   Put their 'bit' on, of course.

Also the festive Queensland bloke,
   The Gulf-man with the gray,
Who grumbled, as he backed his moke,
   "'Twas money thrown away!'

Then stable doors were locked with care,
   The nags long since were fed,
And all the talk and talent there
   Rose up and rolled to bed.

      *   *   *

Oh, fine and fair the morning broke,
   The breeze blew fresh and free,
And all the hard-faced racing folk
   Were on the course to see

Mick's chestnut do a final spin
   Before the sunrise shone;
They knew the Crusoe colt *must* win
   And had their money *on*!

Mick Greenhide saddled up the crack,
   The girths he tightly drew,
And Billy o'er the horse's back
   His off leg nimbly threw.

Alas, the woe that chanced that day,
   When Mick let go his head
The colt refused to go away,
   But 'gan to buck instead.

Oh, he bucked up! and he bucked down
   And mightily bucked he!
And all the talent of the town
   Were on the course to see!

At first, the people thought it sport.
   Bill didn't think that same;
A four pound roller ain't the sort
   Of saddle for *that* game.

The colt bucked up an awful height,
   Mick cried: 'Stick to him, Bill!'
Said 'Brumby,' breathlessly, 'Alright,
   Whilst I can stick, I *will*!'

The roller, as he spoke turned round
   And, with a backward buck,
The horse hurled William to the ground, —
   'Twas really awful luck!

From many a loud blaspheming tongue
   Went up a doleful shout,
As punters saw the jockey 'slung,'
   And watched Mick's colt clear out.

As swirls the dust-storm o'er the plains
   About the parched Barcoo,
With roller turned and streaming reins,
   The frantic race-horse flew.

At once of mounted men, a batch
   Hied off in hot pursuit,
But never a nag had pace to catch
   The flying bucking brute.

The sun blazed down as hot as h-ll,
   What time the race was run;
Mick brought him back to Bidgeebel
   In time to learn 'what won'.

The Handicap was won that day,
   And punters looked askance,
The Gulf-man won it with his gray—
   The nag that had no chance!

To him—who owned the speedy gray—
   They paid the money o'er;
He bade the Bidgee Boys 'Good-day!'
   And cleared—for evermore!

Next day they to the saddler took
   The roller—for repair!
Grimly his head the saddler shook
   On finding in the hair

Which stuffed the roller, short sharp nails—
   Which same said he revealed
How 'twas against the race-course rails
   The colt had bucked and squealed.

Now stockmen, o'er their whisky, tell
   Queer yarns about that chap
Who came along to Bidgeebel
   And sneaked the Handicap.

They 'dropped'—that he whose horse out-paced
   Their nags of New South Wales
Had somehow in Mick's roller placed
   Those d--d and dreadful nails.

And Goorybibil fellows swore
   That whereso'er they see—
They'll raise his crimson hair who wore
   The moles and cabbage-tree!

'BE SENSIBLE' — A MORAL

'Be sensible!' fair Nelly said —
   Her bright eyes glancing slyly —
As Jack, with mistletoe o'erhead,
   Essayed to kiss her shyly.

'Withdraw your arm, sir, from my waist!'
   And Jack, thus being chidden,
Ceased spooning, and in shameful haste
   Waxed 'sensible,' as bidden.

'Be sensible!' fair Nelly cried
   In tones of piteous wailing,
But found, when Dick to kiss her tried,
   All protest unavailing.

'Be sensible and stop! Ah, do!'
   Whereon the rascal clever,
Remarked, 'Why, sweetheart Nell, with you
   I fain would "stop" for ever!'

      *   *   *   *

'Each time I bade Dick "stop"' mused Nell,
   'The rascal kissed me twice.
He'd not be sensible, but — well,
   I found him vastly nice,
Whilst as for Jack — I fear that he
   Knows little love of Cupid —
He *did* get "sensible" you see,
   And, Oh! I thought him stupid.'

Morant's feelings for women seem from his verses to have veered between an affection for some on a short-term basis ('Love me much a little while') to a quite bitter dislike of others as shrews ('Two Gossips'), as unfeminine ('A Striking Girl'), or as untrustworthy ('Rule Nisi'); although there are a number of poems in the fully romantic vein, love poems like 'Parlez Doucement', 'Where Willow-trees fringe a Fairyland', and the very touching 'At Last'.

But, again from his writings, his truer feelings seem to have centred on the close friendships of a few men like Ogilvie, his droving mate Pat Magee, and some of his army comrades — and his horses. He wrote lovingly of Cavalier and Harlequin in poems and in correspondence, and it is part of the contrary character of the man that, with all that obvious affection, he was willing to use his horses unsparingly and put them at high jumps from bad take-offs for no more than a bar-room bet.

Returning for a moment to the business of The Breaker's birthright, consider part of an article written in 1902 for the old *Windsor and Richmond Gazette*. The writer calls himself only 'The Breaker's Mate' and he begins by saying, as from personal knowledge, 'It may not be known that the late Lieut. H. H. Morant, "The Breaker", took his first riding lessons on the knee of the Devonshire sport and author, G. J. Whyte-Melville. Poor Morant. (His tutor was) Hot-headed, violent at times (and) a great horseman. He jolted the hard-faced youngster up and down, and on his head he put a hunting-cap, and in his chubby hand a riding crop, then man and boy rode a great burst over imaginary fences, with a "Tally Ho!" for a finish. Morant was very reserved, but at times he talked to this sorrowing mate of Devonshire and childhood, when at eight years of age he rode to hounds.'

The writer then goes on to list yet more of Morant's daredevil riding feats and mentions that he introduced polo to the Hawkesbury River district. Finally, after referring to Admiral Morant's denial of any connection with Harry, he ends by saying: 'The present writer can hardly reconcile himself to the statement, having seen two letters written to Morant by his mother and sister, one being dated from Naples, the other from Marseilles. In the latter family matters were touched upon, and left no doubt in my mind as to his identity. Harry Morant also had in his possession some souvenirs, among which was a ring, given him by the girl he was engaged to, and a cigar-holder with his mother's name thereon. I was with Morant when he interviewed a lawyer, and prevailed upon him to write to the irreconcilable Admiral and intercede for him. Will Ogilvie, at present in England, and others, could bear out the writer's statement also if he cared to.'

By the turn of the century Harry Morant had lived and worked in Australia for more than fifteen years and the hard life and drink had taken the fine edge off him. He was closing the gap towards forty by then; a short, wide-shouldered, and muscular man with a horseman's gait, a sharp look, and a thrusting jaw. It is likely that the Boer War was, for him, no more than a new adventure, a change of the pace which must have become dreary to him. He enlisted for South Africa and sailed as a Lance-Corporal in the Second Contingent, the South Australian Mounted Rifles, his name showing on the nominal roll for some reason as Henry Horland Morant—probably the result of hasty

This previously unpublished photograph shows The Breaker (centre) when he was a member of the 2nd South Australian Mounted Rifles (*Photo: South Australian Archives*)

transliteration from an equally hasty signature. The contingent sailed on 26 January 1900 and landed at the Cape on 25 February, almost exactly two years before he was to face a firing party.

By the time Morant's contingent disembarked he was a sergeant and already something of a personality among the troops, known to many for his horsemanship and to others for his verses in the *Bulletin* as well. He obviously took to the life and the change of pace from his drifting and drinking days and he soon fell into an area of occupation for which he was perfectly suited.

In the move up with French's cavalry to relieve Kimberley and in the hard and fighting advance to Paardeburg it became painfully clear that good horses were in increasingly short supply. The mounts which had come with the Australians were thinned out badly by deaths and wounds and sickness; their replacements were of poor quality—ill-bred animals from the Argentine mostly—or were shipped into South Africa unbroken and savage from the long journey. Morant, like many other Australians, had a flair for dealing with the wild horses and 'finding' others of better quality, and it soon enough became common knowledge that 'The Breaker' wasn't called that for nothing. Perhaps 'The Taker' might have been as good a name, for Staff horses and any others of any quality were never safe; in the Wild West of America Harry Morant might well have ended his time at the end of a rustler's rope.

Word filtered through the entire command and French himself got to hear of this Australian mounted infantryman who could not only comport himself in a gentlemanly manner but also could dash off lines of verse, 'find'—and sell—useful polo ponies, and provide mules and horses almost at call. Morant found himself attached to the Staff as a galloper (a despatch-rider) and was at once in an atmosphere which suited him very well. There was none of the grind of the line, better rations and some drink to be had, easier lying at night, and enough excitement spiced with danger to add to the glamour of being a Staff galloper. There was also the extra money to be had in the sale of ponies to officers about the headquarters.

In mid-June 1900 the London *Daily Telegraph* war correspondent Bennet Burleigh was introduced to Harry Morant. Burleigh was short of a rider to carry his despatches, and here was a man who could not only do that, and do it superbly well, but who was amusing, literate, and who knew his way around both headquarters and the Australian units. For something more than six months the two men were inseparable, moving companionably from the front to the fleshpots of Cape Town. It was a period which covered Burleigh's running foul of his paper for expressing some sympathy with the

Major-General French, a skilful and respected cavalry leader (*Photo: Australian War Memorial*)

Boer cause, Lord Roberts relinquishing command and sailing for England, and the expiry of the time of enlistment for the 2nd South Australians. They sailed for home in October of 1900 and their Officer Commanding, Major Reade, wrote a farewell letter to Morant in which he praised his conduct, his soldierly behaviour, and continual alertness, and went on to say that these commendations were endorsed by all the officers of the regiment.

A little after this Burleigh was recalled to London. Morant, his interesting and congenial job ended and his regiment gone, took his discharge and his savings, arranged for the free passage to which he was entitled, and sailed with Burleigh for England.

The three or four months Harry Morant spent 'at Home' only add to the mystery of his background. There is no concrete evidence of his movements, only what has been said and written by a number of people, some of them of that time. Yet there is a similarity about these reports—between them they cover the same sort of ground: that he went down into Devonshire; that he rode in the right county-social set with Mark Rollo's staghounds; that he met and became fast

London *Daily Telegraph* war correspondent Bennet Burleigh, for whom Harry Morant was a despatch-rider (*Photo: Illustration Research Service*)

friends with a Hussar officer, Captain Frederick Hunt; that he fell in love. There is a quite unsubstantiated story that he and Hunt were engaged to marry a pair of sisters. Given that he *was* Harry Harbord Morant, the well-bred, exiled son of a county family, he could be expected to move in those circles; it is much less likely that Edwin Henry Murrant, son of a workhouse-master, could have got away with it.

Whatever the truth of that English interval may have been, in South Africa there were unassailable facts. Kitchener was in command and the swing of the year brought with it his urgent calls for more men, more horses, and a more relentless pursuit of the Boers. For both Morant and Hunt the call was irresistible. Neither seems to have been the sort of man for whom the social round (the 'poodle-faking') would have held a long appeal; and for Morant, well, perhaps he had made his point in going back to England, in being for a while the man he believed he should have been. Without doubt he had enjoyed the year he had spent in South Africa and could see an extension of that enjoyment, could probably see advancement and excitement ahead. The time was right for his next move.

Hunt went first and by the time Morant reached the Cape there was a message waiting for him telling him about the formation of the Bush Veldt Carbineers. The attraction was immediate. The BVC seemed likely to offer the degree of freedom from formality which matched well with Morant's nature: it was to operate where there was action; he could, at one bound, become an officer and, by formal military recognition, a gentlèman; the commander under whom he would serve was Lenehan, a man known to him from old times in Australia.

The Breaker became Lieutenant Morant, BVC, on April Fool's Day 1901. He then had less than eleven months to live.

4

Court Martial

It seems to have become common to refer to 'The Court Martial' of the BVC officers, placing a false interpretation of singleness on what was actually a series of trials. I plead guilty to fostering this impression, and the producers and director of the film *Breaker Morant* must share some part of that guilt. For dramatic reasons the trials were more easily handled in the novel and the film when taken as a whole, as though the men on trial were being charged and dealt with for some single, overall crime. There were, in fact, several crimes on the charge sheets and, while the men were tried jointly, each case was heard individually and the whole series was preceded by a Court of Inquiry to establish that there was reason to go further.

The only eyewitness account we have of the arrests of the men comes from one of them, from George Witton, who appears to have been the last one picked up. When he arrived at Pietersburg from up-country he was asked to report to the Garrison Commandant, Colonel Hall, after which he was handed over to a junior officer and told that he was under close arrest pending a Court of Inquiry. By that time Morant, Handcock, and Picton were already being held under close arrest, as were Major Lenehan, their Commanding Officer, Captain Taylor, the Field Intelligence Officer, and Lieutenant Hannam and Sergeant-Major Hammett, both of the BVC. They were segregated from one another and held in close confinement.

The 1899 edition of the Manual of Military Law states in Chapter IV that 'an officer placed under arrest should always be informed in writing of the nature of the arrest . . .' and, in Section 4, 'As a rule, a commanding officer will not place an officer under arrest without investigation of the complaint or the circumstances tending to criminate him; though cases may occur where it may be necessary to do so.'

There is now no documentation to show precisely what happened then but from George Witton the impression is firm that there was precious little prior investigation and none of the prisoners was informed in writing of the reasons for his arrest. Major-General Sir David Hughes-Morgan, Bt, CBE, Director of Legal Services at the Ministry of Defence has commented to me, 'I really cannot say what happened if an officer was placed in arrest in the field, the circumstances are so varied that it is probably impossible to do more than guess. The only stipulation then in force regarding delay in bringing an arrested person to trial was in Army Act 1881 S45 which required a report to be made every eight days. This did not apply however on active service.'

It appears that the men were arrested, held closely and separately, possibly without being advised in writing of the reasons, and that they were kept like that for some time before appearing at the Court of Inquiry. That Court was convened under the Presidency of Colonel Carter of the Wiltshire Regiment, the two Members of the Court being officers of the same regiment, and it was during those preliminary proceedings that the arrested men discovered the nature of the charges they were to face.

There seemed to be plenty of reasons for inquiry when the court settled down to look at the reported events of the preceding three months. In July 1901 the Bush Veldt Carbineers had been established in the Spelonken for no more than three or four weeks, based on Fort Hendrina (which they renamed Fort Edward) and under the command of Captain Robertson, a young English officer with somewhat dandyish affectations. Peter Handcock was with that detachment.

In those first few weeks the BVC settled into a routine of fairly limited patrols, learning something of the tough territory which surrounded them and discovering that the Boers raiding the railway line which ran through it were as tough as the country, and very difficult to pin down. The troopers also found that Robertson was no disciplinarian and they took advantage of the fact. There was a deal of drunkenness and theft, and some cases of rape, but Robertson took little notice of the complaints of the locals, white and native, as long as his men could saddle up and ride, however shoddily. He was a weak and ineffectual man and he came under the powerful influence of Captain Alfred Taylor.

Taylor was an Irish-born South African whose many years of experience in the country as a guide and soldier led to his being attached to the army's Intelligence Staff. He had an unsavoury reputation as a ruthless and sadistic man — indeed, the native name

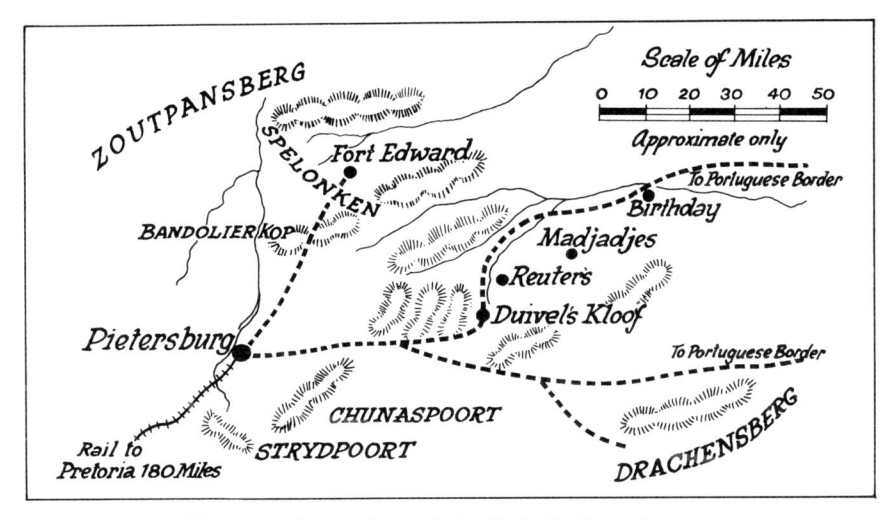

The area of operations of the Bush Veldt Carbineers

for him was 'Bulala' which meant 'Killer'. Nonetheless he was extremely knowledgeable and fluent in languages and dialects of the natives, and there was logic in his being sent to the Spelonken as Area Commandant. This was not, properly speaking, a military command but was more concerned with direct Intelligence work, with gathering and passing on information about Boer bands in the district, and assisting in restricting their supplies. Taylor, it seems clear, saw it as part of his job to take a rather more direct hand in things.

While this Intelligence officer has always been something of a shadow-figure in what has previously been written and filmed, he needs to be kept clearly in mind—for he held quite considerable sway, not just with the junior officers of the BVC but with the Commanding Officer, Major Lenehan, for whom he acted on some occasions as second-in-command at Headquarters.

When word came to Fort Edward that a party of Boers was heading in to surrender it was Taylor, not Robertson, who took command. He sent out a patrol to meet the two wagons in which the Boers were reported to be travelling, a patrol with some definite instructions. When the wagons were sighted the patrol fired on them. White flags of surrender were shown and the patrol commander, Sergeant Oldham, moved his men in to see whether there were women or children with the party. There were only six men, one of them lying grievously ill inside a wagon, and Oldham, apparently obeying Taylor's explicit orders that no prisoners were to be taken, had them all shot out of hand, the sick man being killed where he lay.

In that patrol was Trooper Van Buren, a young Boer who had changed sides some time earlier and who had become a Carbineer. He was shocked at the wanton slaughter, made the fact plain and, when he was later seen talking with the widows of the dead men after they had been brought into the fort, it was assumed that he had told them what had happened. Plainly, if that was the case, he was a danger to all those who had taken part, and most especially to Taylor who had ordered the patrol.

Lieutenant Handcock—again on orders from Taylor, supported by Robertson—took out another patrol with Van Buren as one of its members. Handcock placed the young trooper well out on the left flank where there was heavy scrub and rode after him. A little later there was a brief burst of pistol fire and Handcock rode back in, saying that Van Buren had been shot by Boers. His report on the incident, re-written by Robertson, was sent to Pietersburg as the official version.

By that time the laxity at Fort Edward had become known in Pietersburg and Lenehan decided to send Captain Hunt up to replace Robertson who, a little later, was dismissed from military service.

A Boer guard detail coming off duty with their sleeping gear (*Photo: Australian War Memorial*)

Hunt took his friend Morant with him and they were followed by two other officers—Lieutenants Hannam and Picton—and the troopers of the BVC suddenly found a very different set of circumstances prevailing. Hunt was a regular British officer, a Hussar, and he at once set about bringing his men into line, cutting out the drinking which had left many of them unfit for action, destroying some illicit stills, returning stolen cattle and property to their owners, and restoring a measure of soldierly discipline. The locals may have been properly grateful but it is certain that Hunt was less than popular with many of his own men, and the unpopularity extended to Harry Morant who was Hunt's enthusiastic supporter.

By August, when a reinforcement troop was sent up from Pietersburg, conditions at Fort Edward were considerably more formal and there was regular and effective patrolling going on. Captain Taylor, while still exercising some measure of control, found it much harder to sway Hunt than he had Robertson, but the two men rubbed along well enough together. The reinforcements were led into the fort by Lieutenant Witton and, for the first time, the four central characters in the impending tragedy were together.

It is some indication of the scope of the BVC's operations that Hunt should decide to mount an action against a group of Boers close to 160 kilometres from Fort Edward. Duivel's Kloof was a farm used as a base by a Boer commander, Field-Cornet Viljoen, and from it he and his men raided widely, striking not only at the railway line and British outposts but also at the properties of the few Boers who fought for or supported the British. One of those was Frank Eland, a BVC sergeant whose farm at Raven's Hill had been a frequent target for Viljoen. Word came in that Viljoen and his commandos were 'at home' and that a party of Boers had ambushed and held siege to one of the BVC patrols. Hunt determined to rescue his men and to attack Duivel's Kloof, and in the ensuing firefight both he and Sergeant Eland were killed.

When Morant, Handcock, Witton, and Picton arrived the next morning with a large fighting patrol the small battle was over, the Boers had fled, and Morant found that Hunt's body had been mutilated. He sank into a morose and killing rage over the death and disfigurement of his friend and in the weeks that followed, through the rest of August and into September, the raids he led were both successful and vengeful. He attacked a Boer encampment shortly after Hunt's death and took prisoner Josef Visser who, it was claimed, was wearing some of Hunt's clothes. Against all military regulations Morant set up a drumhead court martial and had Visser shot, Picton administering the *coup de grâce* with a revolver. This killing was reported by Morant to his Commanding Officer, Major Lenehan.

A week or two later a BVC patrol took eight or nine prisoners and began leading them towards the fort, but were met a few kilometres out by Morant, riding with Handcock, Witton, and a small troop. Morant took over the prisoners and sent the patrol in to Fort Edward, keeping with him his fellow officers and three troopers, one of whom was a loyalist Boer, Theunis Botha. Between them they shot the prisoners to death along the roadside. The bodies were still warm when a small cart driven by a German missionary, Daniel Heese, drove along the road with those corpses in plain view. After being halted by Morant and warned not to go further—towards possible Boer raiders—the missionary was allowed to go on his way and was later found shot to death. Handcock and Morant had been in close conversation as the missionary left them and Handcock was then seen to ride out, armed with a carbine, in the same general direction.

The catalogue of grim events was not over. The Court of Inquiry also heard how a patrol led by Lieutenant Hannam had apparently fired on a group of Boers and killed children, but the supporting evidence was sketchy. Much more definite, however, was the report

The original grave of Captain Hunt, buried at Reuters Mission Station, Medingen. His remains have been moved to the Garden of Remembrance in Pietersburg (*Photo: South African War Graves Board*)

This picture shows the typical adaptability of Australians in times of war—or, 'living off the land' (*Photo: Australian War Memorial*)

that three Boers, one of them a twelve-year-old boy, had tried to surrender and had been killed by a BVC patrol led by Morant, with Handcock and Witton riding with him.

But by the time the court came to consider that, Harry Morant was away out into the bush again, this time chasing a notorious Boer leader, Commandant Tom Kelly. It was a chase which led right across the Spelonken and close to Portuguese Territory and it was successful. Kelly was taken by surprise by the fast-moving Morant who led his captive back to Pietersburg where he sought and was granted two weeks leave. It was on his return from that dip into the fleshpots that he was arrested and joined the others under tight guard.

The outcome of the Court of Inquiry was that there was enough evidence against the Bush Veldt Carbineers' officers to institute courts martial on a number of counts. Major Lenehan was charged with culpable neglect on omitting to make a report which it was his duty to make. Morant, Handcock, Picton, and Witton were all charged with the murder of the prisoner, Visser. All but Picton were charged with the murder of eight Boers. Morant and Handcock were further charged with the murder of three Boers on another occasion and Handcock alone faced yet another charge, of murdering a German missionary; Morant was charged with instigating and commanding that killing. Peter Handcock was also charged with murdering one of his own troopers, Van Buren. In addition to all that, Captain Alfred Taylor was charged with the murder of six men.

At this point there are things I want to make clear. At the time I wrote my novel, *The Breaker*, I was concerned to write a good story, to write it as well as I could, and to put into it the sorts of marketable factors for which plain professionalism called. I had been given the elements of an exciting tale, with a bold and intriguing central character, and I had spent some considerable time and all the money I could afford in trying to find out as much as possible about both. It was not a successful search since it was done piecemeal, because of the need for me to leave the task frequently in order to earn a living and because I was working without the assistance of publicity. I wrote a draft screenplay as a piece of imaginative fiction based on some known facts, a good deal of hearsay, and some legends; a publisher read it and contracted me to write a book from that screenplay.

By then I was financially unable to go any further with research and I took the chance gladly—but the story nagged at me so that, in the years following, I kept at it whenever I could. Now, almost twelve years after I first began working at it and because of the interim success of the novel and the film, widespread publicity has put me in touch with an extraordinarily diverse body of people. From them has come material which I had hunted uselessly that long time ago, and that material has shown me that, however interesting and popular my novel may have become, its emphases and suggestions were in many cases wide of the mark.

Whatever politics may have dictated, whatever the relationships of the military and the government, it is extremely unlikely that any British military court would have been pressured to bring down a directed verdict. Cold logic dictates that even if one officer as a Member or as President of such a court could have been influenced, there is virtually no chance that a number of professional officers could have been so swayed. Aside from anything else the social code under which such men at that time lived would have precluded any suggestion of corrupt practice, of 'not playing the game', and the military code could do no more than reinforce that attitude.

Certainly there are inconsistencies in the overall conduct of the cases against the accused BVC officers and there are unanswered questions about the motives of Kitchener in some of his actions. None of that is sufficient to alter my present belief that the trials themselves were conducted as fairly and fully as was possible, given that the men sitting in judgment were not legally trained, that they had their personal biases as well as their military ones, and that they heard grossly conflicting evidence and had to find their way to what they saw as the truth. And it was all done under conditions of war in the field.

For all the time since I first heard about the execution of Breaker Morant and until very recently I have tried to find a copy of the transcript of the proceedings of the courts martial. In London some years ago I was given a variety of answers to my questions as to the whereabouts of those papers, and the differences in the answers—from destruction by enemy air-raid to their never having been received—left me with the firm impression that I was being misled for some reason or another. Now I believe that the only accurate answer I was given was that the documents had been destroyed.

From Diana Birch, a researcher in London, comes this information: 'I searched the indexes to the original correspondence,

---

DIANA BIRCH RESEARCH SERVICES
90 Dartmouth Road Forest Hill London SE23 01-699 0914

SEARCH REPORT

I searched the indexes to the original correspondence, South Africa with the Colonial Office. I found some references to the cases you refer to. There were about 4 easily identifiable entries and possibly one or two others might have been of interest. Unfortunately the documents have been 'destroyed under statute' hence are not available. I gather from the short entries given in the indexes that the cases were discussed in Parliament. Can I assume that you have seen copies of the Parliamentary proceedings? I could get copies although they are not kept at the Public Record Office which is where I usually work.

A photostat copy of the search report of Diana Birch, engaged by the author to ferret out information

South Africa with the Colonial Office. I found some references to the cases you refer to. There were about 4 easily identifiable entries and possibly one or two others might have been of interest. Unfortunately the documents have been *"destroyed under statute" . . .'* (my italics). That report went to Dr Dick Schulenberg of Pretoria, a keen historian, and he followed up the reference to that destruction by writing to the Public Record Office in Kew. The following is the response.

21 September 1981

'Dear Dr Schulenburg

"Destroyed under statute" is a phrase used to describe destruction of records under the powers granted by the Public Record Office Act of 1877 by which schedules were drawn up of types of record held by departments and courts not suitable for permanent preservation, with the periods after which they might be disposed of. The Act ceased to have effect at the end of 1958 when the current Public Records Act came into force.

Courts Martial proceedings appear on a schedule of July 1922 which has a general proviso that matter likely to be of value as precedent or to be of historical, technical or legal importance was to be withdrawn for preservation but it does not appear that this was done. *No War Office Court Martial proceedings now survive for the period between 1850 and 1914* with the exception of one single case in 1879. *The arrangements current since 1958, which have operated on the post 1913 proceedings, would have seen to the survival of the Hancock and Morant papers, but regrettably the errors of past practice cannot now be recovered.*

Yours sincerely
Nicholas Cox
Head of Search Department, Kew'

In 1921, J. F. Thomas wrote a letter to the Mitchell Library and in a final note he said, "It may (be) of some little interest to note also that I have the whole of the proceedings of the Courts Martial held at Pietersburg, correspondence, etc." In two visits to Tenterfield, where he wrote that letter, I've searched the offices and building of the "Star" newspaper and gone through several boxes of Thomas' papers in a nearby solicitor's rooms without success. Every attempt to locate his brother, who was a witness to the registry of his death, was useless. No-one now alive who knew him knows where those papers are, and the feeling is now strong upon me that they're never going to be found, that there is now no immediate evidence of or report on the proceedings of those distant and dramatic trials. Except

George Ramsdale Witton photographed in 1930, three years after publication of his book *Scapegoats of the Empire* (Photo: *Australian War Memorial*)

for the version given in George Witton's book "Scapegoats of the Empire" in which he offers his own recollections of those tense times—and one other. Witton, writing in the late 1920's exhibits remarkable recall when setting out testimony and questioning or— more likely—he somehow retained or got notes and papers relevant to what happened. But it's difficult to forget that he was one of the accused men, that he suffered greatly afterwards and that he was for ever after biased in his attitudes. The one other report I've found is, I feel, much more likely to be dispassionate since it's quite unlikely that a professional reporter would have felt the need to lean in one direction or the other. I have taken out a few passages which have no immediate bearing on the report, and made a few minor changes in spelling and punctuation. All the material shown in brackets is my own and in many places I have replaced the word "witness" with the name of the man concerned. In no case is the sense of the material changed from the original. Aside from these things, here is the text of what was published in the London "Daily Telegraph" of Thursday, April 17th., 1902.

> Reuter's correspondent, writing from Durban on March 22, furnishes the following detailed account of the trial by general court-martial, which began at Pietersburg (Transvaal) on Jan. 17, 1902. This, of

course, is the case which has aroused so much painful interest throughout the British Empire. The correspondent says the court was composed of Lieutenant-Colonel Denny (president) and five other officers. Major Copland was Judge-Advocate, and Captain Burn-Begg, Public Prosecutor.

The prisoners were charged with the murder of a wounded Boer prisoner named Visser. They pleased not guilty, and were defended by Major Thomas, New South Wales Mounted Rifles.

The prosecution called Sergeant S. Robertson, who stated that he remembered the fight at Devil's Kloof, when Captain Hunt was killed. Captain Hunt's body was found to have been stripped. He took the bodies back to Reuter's Farm where the party was reinforced by Lieutenants Morant, Handcock, Picton and Witton.

Next morning they went in pursuit of the Boers, overtook them and captured their laager, finding one wounded Boer there. Next day the Boer accompanied the force some distance. During the dinner hour the accused held a conversation in which the Boer prisoner who was in a Cape Cart six yards away appeared to take no part. Morant and an intelligence officer named Ledeboer went to Visser (the Boer prisoner) telling him they were sorry, but that he had been found guilty of being in possession of the late Captain Hunt's clothing and also of wearing khaki.

Robertson did not catch what further was said but was told to warn two men for duty. He refused, asking Picton by whose orders this man was to be shot. Picton replied that the orders were by Lord Kitchener, naming a certain date, and were to the effect that all Boers wearing khaki from that date were to be shot. Robertson said he had never seen such orders, which should have been posted or read regimentally.

Cross-examined he said Captain Hunt's body bore marks of ill-treatment. The prisoner had a kind of khaki jacket on. Captain Hunt had previously told Robertson that he had direct orders that no prisoners were to be taken. On one occasion Captain Hunt abused Robertson for bringing in three prisoners against orders. Morant had previously been considerate to prisoners. He was in charge of the firing party that executed Visser.

Trooper Botha corroborated the previous witness and said he was one of the firing party who carried out the sentence on Visser, who was carried down to a river and shot. Botha had previously lived with Visser on the same farm. He objected to forming one of the firing party.

Corporal Sharp also corroborated and said that after the firing party had fired Picton discharged his revolver, apparently at the dead man's head.

L. Ledeboer (the intelligence officer previously mentioned) deposed that on August 10 last year he translated the sentence of a court-martial that condemned Visser to be shot. Morant, Handcock, Picton and Witton formed the court-martial.

Prisoners elected to give evidence on their own behalf.

Morant stated that he was under Captain Hunt with the force charged with clearing the northern district of Boers. It was regular guerilla warfare. Captain Hunt acted on orders he brought from Pretoria. On one occasion Morant brought in thirty prisoners, when Captain Hunt reprimanded him for bringing them in at all and told him not to do it again. Morant took command after Captain Hunt was killed and went with reinforcements. When he learnt the circumstances of Captain Hunt's death, and the way he had been maltreated, he followed the Boers and attacked their laager. The Boers cleared, leaving Visser who had on a soldier's shirt and was using Captain Hunt's trousers as a pillow. He was court-martialled and shot on this account. The others knew of Captain Hunt's orders. Morant told them he had previously disregarded them, but after the way the Boers had treated Captain Hunt he would carry out the orders which he regarded as lawful.

   Cross-examined, Morant said Captain Hunt's orders were to clear Spelonken and take no prisoners. He had never seen those orders in writing. Captain Hunt quoted the action of Kitchener's and Strathcona's Horse as precedents. Morant had not previously carried out the orders because his captures were 'a good lot'. He had shot no prisoners prior to Visser.

   Morant was asked whether he knew who gave the orders but the Judge-Advocate protested against the question and was upheld by the Court after consultation. On the resumption of the trial next day however the Court allowed the question and prisoner Morant stated that Colonel Hamilton, Military Secretary, was the one who had given Captain Hunt the orders that no prisoners were to be taken. Others received those orders from Captain Hunt, including Handcock.

   The Court-martial (of Visser) was reported to Colonel Hall (Commander, Lines of Communication, Northern District) within a fortnight after it was held. A report was also sent to Captain Taylor. Morant had only Captain Hunt's word for it that Colonel Hamilton had given those orders. Morant had made no attempt to get his report of the court-martial as evidence.

   Picton, another of the accused, deposed that after the capture of Visser, Morant said that he was perfectly justified in shooting him. Picton said it would be hard lines to shoot him and asked Morant to call the other officers together. A meeting was held and it was decided to shoot Visser. Picton corroborated the statement that he also had received orders from Captain Hunt not to take prisoners. He never questioned the orders and had been reprimanded by Hunt for bringing in prisoners. Picton reported the execution of Visser to Major Lenehan verbally, immediately after, and then to Colonel Hall. Morant and Hunt had been old friends and after Hunt's death Morant was inclined to be more severe to the enemy. Picton had never previously shot a prisoner or seen one shot. Visser was not informed of the nature of the trial that was taking place. Picton opposed the shooting of Visser at the court-martial. He had never obeyed the order to take no prisoners because he did not like the idea. He was in command of the firing party and merely obeyed orders.

Major Neatson, staff officer to Colonel Hall, deposed that he had received certain reports from Captain Taylor re engagements with Boers, but remembered nothing about a summary of a court-martial.

P. J. Handcock, another of the prisoners, deposed that he had attended the trial of Visser at Morant's request. He corroborated the previous evidence as to the reason for executing Visser and the orders not to take prisoners.

Prisoner Witton also corroborated and said he was present at a conversation with a Mr. Reuter from which he gathered that Hunt had been murdered. Reuter said Hunt's neck had been broken and his eyes gouged out. Witton was guided by his superior officers in regard to the finding of the court-martial. He believed Visser knew that he was being tried but he was given no opportunity to speak or make a defence.

F. L. Reuter, missionary in charge of the German Berlin Missionary Station, deposed that Captain Hunt's body was brought to his place and was much mutilated. The neck appeared to have been broken and the face bore marks of boot-nails.

Civil Surgeon Johnston testified that he had heard Hunt reprimand Morant for bringing in prisoners. He was of opinion from the evidence that the injuries to Hunt's body were caused before death.

Major Lenehan, in command of the Bushveld Carbineers, was next called.

He said he had no direct control over the corps, which acted under headquarters at Pretoria. Captain Taylor took command from Captain Robertson and got orders from the officer commanding the line of communications.

Major Bolton (Provost Major, Pietersburg) denied any knowledge of a proclamation that Boers taken in khaki were to be shot.

The evidence of Colonel Hamilton, taken in Pretoria, emphatically denied the issue of any order that no prisoners were to be taken.

On the 23rd. the Court sat to hear the case against Major Lenehan. The charge against him was that, being on active service, he culpably neglected his duty by failing to report the shooting by men of his regiment of one man and two boys, these being prisoners and unarmed. Lenehan pleaded not guilty.

Trooper Botha deposed that three Boers were being brought in by Captain Taylor's Police, and were shot at close quarters by five of his corps. Botha reported what had been done to Morant in presence of Lenehan. Trooper Boony testified to hearing the last witness make his report to Morant.

In his defence the accused denied having heard any such report made to Morant.

The accused was further charged with having failed to report that a trooper of the Bushveld Carbineers had been shot by Lieutenant Handcock. He pleaded not guilty.

Lieutenant Edwards deposed that he received a confidential letter from Captain Hunt of which a copy was made, the original being forwarded to Pretoria. A postscript to the original had since been torn off. The postscript read 'Will also write details of death of Van Burens. Handcock shot him.' The detachment in which Van Burens was only nominally a detachment of the corps. No details of Van Burens' death were ever received. Lenehan sent word by the witness, Edwards, that he would make a confidential report. It was Handcock himself who reported the death of Van Burens.

Major Bolton gave evidence as to searching Lenehan's kit and finding the letter produced, minus the footnote.

Ex-Captain Robertson said he knew Van Burens who was shot on July 4 last. He had been warned about him as one not to be trusted. Robertson, Taylor and Handcock had a talk over the man and it was decided he was to be shot. Handcock and four men went out on the left flank and, when it was finished, Robertson told Lenehan. The report made to Lenehan of Van Burens' death was not a true one. Robertson concealed the true facts in the interest of the corps. Taylor and Hunt also knew the true facts.

The accused, Lenehan, in his defence denied that Robertson had ever informed him of the manner of Van Burens' death. It never occurred to him that the postscript in Hunt's letter intended anything suspicious.

Captain Taylor denied being party to the conversation when it was agreed that Van Burens must be shot. Robertson had mentioned casually that he would have to shoot him, but Taylor never heard till afterwards that he had been shot.

Lieutenant Handcock denied that a meeting was held which decided on the shooting of Van Burens. He had carried out Robertson's instructions in this matter and Robertson ordered him to report, making it appear that Van Burens had been shot in a brush with the Boers. The report he prepared did not suit Robertson who wrote one himself. Handcock reported the true facts to Hunt, asking him to inform Lenehan. He told Robertson of this and Robertson said he was a fool to have anything put in black and white. Handcock said Robertson's evidence was all a fabrication.

Lieutenants Morant, P. J. Handcock and G. Witton were then charged with the murder of, or with having instigated others to murder, eight men whose names were unknown. They pleaded not guilty. Major Bolton prosecuted.

L. H. Ledeboer (the intelligence officer) deposed that about August 20 last he was in charge of a party who captured eight Boers. He handed the prisoners over to a patrol and did not know what became of them.

Trooper Thompson stated that he and Troopers Duckett and Lucas were sent for by Morant who asked if they knew the late Captain Hunt and if they had seen Lord Kitchener's proclamation to the effect that 'those who take up the sword shall perish by the sword.' The Lord, he added, had delivered eight Boers into their hands and they were going to shoot them. Lucas objected but Morant said, 'I have orders and must obey them, and you are making a mistake if you think you are going to run the show'. On the morning of the 23rd., Thompson saw a party with eight Boers.

Morant gave orders and the prisoners were taken off the road and shot, Handcock finishing off two with his revolver. Morant afterwards told Thompson that they had to play into his hands or they would know what to expect. Thompson said the evidence he had given at the Court of Inquiry was given under pressure and was untrue. He only knew about Hunt's orders by hearsay. He said Witton was present at the execution.

Sergeant-Major Hammett corroborated as to the shooting of the prisoners. Morant informed him on the previous evening that prisoners were being brought in and were to be shot. Hammett asked Morant if he was sure he was not exceeding his orders. Morant replied that he had hitherto ignored them and would do so no longer. The Boer prisoners were first asked to give information about Tom Kelly (a much-hunted Boer commando leader later captured by Harry Morant) and one of them made a rush at Witton and caught him by the jacket, whereupon he was shot dead and all the rest afterwards. Morant had always treated prisoners well until Hunt's death, and then he became a different man altogether. Witton shot the prisoner who seized hold of him.

Sergeant Wrench corroborated and said it afterwards appeared that some objected to the shooting. Morant told Wrench to find out who did not agree and he would soon get rid of them, adding that he had been congratulated by headquarters over the last affair and meant to go on with it.

The prosecution was then closed. Counsel for the defence claimed the discharge of the prisoners on the ground that the charge was not proven and arguing that they should, if anything, be charged with conspiracy. The Court overruled the objection.

Counsel for the defence then said he did not dispute the facts but would call evidence to show (1) the orders received, (2) what the custom was, having regard to the enemy they were fighting, (3) the practices adopted by other irregular corps against an enemy breaking the usages of war.

Lieutenant Hannam stated that when he was a trooper in the Queensland Mounted Infantry, on one occasion at Brookhorst Spruit, in 1900, his squadron took some prisoners of war and was reprimanded by Colonel Cradock for taking them.

Lieutenant B. F. Guy handed in a statement of trains wrecked on the Pietersburg line by Boers.

J. E. Tucker testified to Boers breaking into refugee camps and carrying off 141 inmates.

A group of officers of the Queensland contingent; seated fourth left in the centre row is the commander, Lt-Col. P. H. Ricardo (*Photo: Australian War Memorial*)

Other evidence showed that Captain Hunt gave distinct orders to sergeants not to take prisoners.

Sergeant Walter Ashton deposed to Brabant's Horse receiving orders to take no prisoners in consequence of specific acts of treachery on the part of the Boers.

The Judge-Advocate objected to such evidence as being irrelevant.

Sergeant McArthur testified to seeing one Boer summarily shot for being caught in khaki.

Lieutenant Colin Phillips said the Queensland Mounted Infantry were in disgrace on one occasion for bringing in prisoners caught sniping. Boers caught breaking the customs of war were shot summarily. Instructions were published in orders in Colonel Garrett's column that Boers caught in khaki were to be shot.

Captain King of the Canadian Scouts stated in evidence that Boers guilty of wearing British uniforms, train wrecking or murdering soldiers were dealt with summarily.

Further testimony as to the good character of all the prisoners and their kindheartedness was given, and the case then closed.

Counsel for the defence pleaded justification on the ground that the Boers in that district were gangs of train-wreckers without a head and their conduct had brought reprisals.

The prosecution submitted that the evidence had not been denied. The eight men had been shot.

The Judge-Advocate refuted the plea of justification. The contention that other corps had done similarly did not make two wrongs right.

The court was cleared and, on its reopening, Major Lenehan was asked if he could give evidence regarding the character of the prisoners. He gave an excellent account of the pluck and good services of Morant. Handcock, he said, had an excellent record and was a simple-minded man with a strong sense of duty, obeying orders implicitly. Witton was also a good soldier and good officer.

Lieutenants Morant and Handcock were next charged with murder in instigating the killing of two Boers and one boy, names unknown. They again pleaded not guilty.

Sergeant-Major Hammett deposed that he was one of the patrol which the prisoners accompanied in search of three Boers. It was reported that the Boers were discovered and it was then agreed that when Morant asked, 'Do you know Captain Hunt?' that was to be the signal for shooting them. This was done. The youngest Boer was about 17. Other members of the patrol corroborated this evidence. It was understood that no prisoners were to be taken.

For the defence Morant deposed that he went out to look for the three Dutchmen. He found them and never asked them to surrender, they being Dutchmen with whom they were at war, and belonging to the party who had stripped and mutilated a brother officer who was a friend of his, he had them shot.

Handcock corroborated and gave evidence as to Hunt's orders that no prisoners were to be taken. The Boers in that district were simply a scattered band of marauders.

Counsel for the defence urged that it must have been a matter of military knowledge that the Boers in this district made no pretence whatever of being under a leader or carrying on recognised warfare.

(On Feb. 7 the Military Court sat to hear the charges against Alfred Taylor who was accused of murder in inciting to kill and murder six men, names unknown. Prisoner pleaded not guilty. The evidence for and against Taylor was little different in nature or tone from that in the other cases, yet after deliberation the Court acquitted Taylor.)

On Feb. 17 the court-martial sat to hear a charge of murder preferred against Lieutenant Handcock in having killed Mr. Hesse, a German missionary, while Lieutenant Morant was charged with the offence of inciting to murder.

The prosecution stated that witnesses would be called to prove that on Aug. 23, 1901, Missionary Hesse left Fort Edward for Pietersburg and the motive for killing him was that he had got to know of the killing of eight Boers and was on his way to Pietersburg to report the occurrence when he was shot by Handcock under orders from Morant.

Trooper Phillip deposed that, on Aug. 23 last, he was on duty at

Cossack Post when a Cape cart containing the missionary and a Cape boy was going in the direction of Pietersburg. The missionary showed a pass signed by Captain Taylor. He was greatly agitated, saying there had been a fight that morning and several had been killed, but he did not say whether they were British or Boers.

Corporal Sharp spoke of seeing Morant addressing Heese and afterwards Handcock riding in the same direction as the missionary. It was about ten or eleven a.m. when the missionary went past, and Handcock went about twelve. The latter had a carbine. He did not take the same route as the missionary.

Cross-examined, Sharp admitted going a long way to fetching one Van Rooyen as a witness, who, he thought, was an eyewitness of the killing of the missionary.

He did say he would walk barefoot from Spelonken to Pietersburg to be of the firing party to shoot Morant. He admitted that Handcock had issued an order against soldiers selling their uniforms in consequence of the fact that he, Sharp, had done so.

Two witnesses spoke to Handcock leaving the fort that day with a rifle. He was on a chestnut horse. It was nothing unusual for an officer to carry a rifle.

A native deposed to seeing an armed man on horseback following the missionary. The man was on a brown horse. The witness afterwards heard shots, then saw the dead body of a coloured boy. He took fright and fled. This was about two p.m.

Trooper Thompson testified to seeing the missionary speaking to the eight Boers who were shot.

Other witnesses gave evidence to having seen Heese speak to Taylor while Morant was present after the shooting of eight men.

H. Van Rooyen (the witness brought from afar by Corporal Sharp) gave evidence as to speaking to the Rev. Mr. Hesse on the road about two p.m. Witness trekked on with his wagon until sundown when he saw a man on horseback coming from the direction of Pietersburg. The man turned off the road. Afterwards a man came on foot to the witness. He could not say if it was the same man he had seen on horseback. The man on foot was Handcock who advised the witness to push on as there were Boers about.

Trooper Botha deposed that he was one of the patrol of which Handcock had charge and which found the missionary's body.

The case for the prosecution then closed.

The accused Morant deposed that on Aug. 23 eight Boers, guilty of train wrecking and other crimes were shot by his orders. Hesse spoke to these Boers and was told not to. Afterwards Morant saw Hesse in a cart. He produced a pass signed by Taylor. Morant advised him not to go on to Pietersburg because of the Boers. Hesse said he would chance it, and by the witness's advice he tied a white flag to the cart. Morant then returned to the fort, then went to Taylor's and he afterwards saw

Handcock at the Bristow's house. Morant never suggested anything about killing the missionary. He was on good terms with him.

The accused Handcock made a statement as to his doings on that day. He said he left on foot for the Schiel's house in the morning, taking the road which branches off to the Pietersburg road and then across country. He lunched at Schiel's and then went to Bristow's till dusk, and then back to the fort.

Further witnesses proved that Handcock was at Schiel's and Bristow's when the missionary was shot.

Plainly, this Reuter report in the *Daily Telegraph* is not a full coverage of the trials, but it seems probable that the reporter had access to a full transcript of the proceedings or that he was present in the court for most of the time. In a pamphlet published in Pretoria the dead missionary's background and death are examined. The section which tells briefly of the trial of Morant and Handcock for that killing includes this note: 'It remains striking that only the case of the murder of the missionary took place behind closed doors', and it seems reasonable to assume that accredited pressmen would have had access to the court at other times. So, despite the journalistic compression of the report, it does cover the salient matters within the court and it gives us the chronology of events.

In the years since then some of the material used in evidence has lain hidden in dusty record-boxes in South Africa; some other material was produced only after the trials and the executions, in some cases many years later. It is possible now—for the first time—to look at those things in relation to what went on in the courtroom and to get some clearer idea of what happened to lead to the trials. (As far as the missionary was concerned, by the way, his name was Heese, not Hesse as it appeared in my novel and in the press report. I wasn't the only one confused—almost everyone writing officially at the time of his death and the trials which followed made the same error; the result, I imagine, of somebody's poor handwriting in the first instance.)

There is no mention in the newspaper report of Trooper Edward Powell being called to give evidence in any of the trials, yet I have a deposition which he wrote and signed on 14 October 1901, witnessed by a Captain Bonham and bearing the Provost Marshal, Army Headquarters, stamp. He gives a full account of riding into camp immediately after the slaughter of six Boers and then a detailed account of the preparations for the killing of Visser and the killing itself. It bears out fully the report in the *Daily Telegraph* but omits a significant fact, as does the press report. That fact comes in a statement from Trooper Botha.

An important part of the defence was that Visser was not just wearing khaki but was wearing some of Captain Hunt's clothes, and was therefore taken to be one of the party of Boers responsible for his death and mutilation. Trooper Botha gave evidence that he had been one of the firing-party, that he objected to the shooting, and that he had lived on the same farm as Visser, but the press report makes no mention of the statement written by him in October of the previous year, a statement which includes a major reference to Hunt's clothing. Here is the text of Botha's deposition:

'I Theunis Johannes Botha hereby make oath and swear as follows —

'I generally acted as interpreter for Lt. Morant. On the evening in which Visser was captured I acted in that capacity. I asked Visser at Lt. Morant's request how Capt. Hunt was killed. He replied that he was killed in fair fight shot through the chest. Lt. Morant said his neck was broken. Visser vehemently denied it. Before commencing to ask these questions Lt. Morant said, "If you tell the truth your life will be spared; if you tell lies you will be shot." He then asked as to the plans of the Boers. Visser replied that the Boers did not intend to stay around there (Little Letaba) but were trekking to the Woodbush to rejoin Beyers' commando. I may say here that but for Lt. Morant's own cowardice the whole of the party would have been caught as every other man in the patrol will testify. Instead of going close up as he could have easily done and so closing the cordon he started firing at 2,000 yards and would not go nearer. In brief, Visser answered every question Lt. Morant asked him and answered them truthfully. In the morning similar questions were again asked him by Lt. Morant who again promised to spare his life if he answered truthfully. Visser answered every question truthfully as subsequent events proved.

'When Ledeboer told Visser he was about to be shot I heard Visser remind Lt. Morant through the interpreter that he had his promise to spare his life as he had truthfully answered all his questions. Lt. Morant said, "It is idle to talk, we are going to shoot you", or words to that effect. Visser when captured was wearing a very old and dilapidated British Warm. I am Lt. Morant's orderly and I can testify that he himself wears Capt. Hunt's British Warm and has had it ever since Captain Hunt's death. It was of a different cut from all others and could easily be identified. He also has most of his other clothes. Visser was not dressed in a single article of Capt. Hunt's clothes when he was captured. Lt. Morant's statement that he was dressed in Capt. Hunt's clothes is utterly false.'

At the start of October a long letter was sent to Colonel Hall at Pretoria from non-commissioned officers and men of the BVC detailing and protesting against crimes committed by their officers. The letter (and a subsequent memorandum) is signed by sixty-one men and makes this plea: 'Sir, many of us are Australians who have fought throughout nearly the whole war while others are Africanders who have also fought from Colenso till now. We cannot return home with the stigma of these crimes attached to our names. Therefore we humbly pray that a full and exhaustive enquiry may be made by impartial Imperial officers in order that the truth may be elicited and justice done. Also we beg that all officers and men be kept in camp at Pietersburg till the enquiry is finished. So deeply do we deplore the opprobrium which must be inseparably connected with these crimes that scarcely a man once his time is up can be prevailed on to re-enlist in this corps. Trusting to the credit of the Army you will grant the inquiry we ask.'

The letter includes this section: 'Fabrication of Evidence by Major Lennehan [*sic*]. When Major Lennehan was sent out to hold an enquiry he endeavoured to bounce the troopers into giving evidence which would exonerate the officers. Particularly he tried to make them swear that the wounded Boer prisoner, Visser, shot on Aug. 11th., was wearing the tunic of the late Capt. Hunt whereas the witnesses pointed out that the *clothes of the late Capt. Hunt had been continuously worn by Lt. Morant who was wearing them himself at that moment*. Lt. Morant wore the late Capt. Hunt's British Warm, riding breeches, tunic and leggings.'

It is very possible that this information, sworn and witnessed, was used by the prosecution in court, but no report was made of it in the press. Yet from this material comes a different view of Morant—as a man prepared to lie outside the court and perjure himself inside it and, if Botha is to be believed, as a coward also. So, if Morant felt enough rage at Hunt's death to fabricate a reason for having Visser shot, was the evidence about the mutilating of Hunt's body equally a fabrication?

It has been suggested that while the Boers shot the man it was local natives who attacked the body, whether it was dead or wounded. One version has it that a mob of nearly a hundred natives watched the fight, waited till the Boers had pulled out, and then descended on the bodies of Hunt and Sergeant Frank Eland, abusing them for the purposes of making magic. Dr Dick Schulenberg, drawing on local sources, says 'settlers in the area believe . . . that it was black witch-doctors who came in the night and mutilated the bodies ... and removed body parts for medicine and ritual purposes.'

Yet the testimony of the missionary F. L. Reuter and of several others was that Hunt's neck was broken and that there were marks of boot-nails on his face. There seems to be little chance that natives, especially witch-doctors, would have been wearing hobnailed boots — unless there was a deliberate attempt made by them to implicate the Boers.

Overall, there is ample evidence in the reports from both sides to show that Hunt was killed in the fight and mutilated afterwards. His body was stripped of its clothing and Morant was enraged to the point where he determined to exact vengeance. From that point on it appears clear enough that his methods were crude and savage and that, in Visser's case at least, he probably felt the need to justify himself in the face of some expressed opposition. Once he had used the excuse of seeing Hunt's gear on Visser he was committed to carrying the story through, out of court and in it, on oath.

The killings of the other Boers were neither doubted nor were they denied, only the *reasons* for the killings were in dispute. The following deposition of Trooper Edward Powell covers the deaths of one group of Boers and the shooting of Trooper Van Burens: 'It was customary to take the advance guard from the right of the line but on this particular day they were plucked from all parts of the patrol. Sergeant Oldham was sent ahead with these picked men, I followed with the main body. Presently we came across some wagons in the road and about one hundred head of oxen in splendid condition. I remarked these must be rich Boers. Then I noticed the bodies lying in the road each with a *round right in the forehead*. One in addition to the wound in the forehead had a wound in the neck. At once the feeling came across me that this had not been a fight but a slaughter. Though our men were exactly equal in numbers to the Boers not one had a scratch while all the Boers were killed. Moreover all the Boers were shot in the same place in the forehead. I was absolutely sickened at the sight and rode on as fast as possible. On the day Trooper Van Burens was killed he came up to my fire at breakfast time to grill a steak. He told me he had got into trouble through being more or less down and talking to the Boers *about the slaughter of the six*. He said, "I do not care what the officers say. I will not see murder passed by and nothing said about it." The words were to this effect. Later in the day Lt. Handcock was detached with fourteen of the men one of whom was Van Burens to scout for some Boers alleged to be on the left. Captain Taylor was in charge of the whole patrol and Captain Robertson was also present.

A far cry from the Officers' Mess is the humpy shelter for this Bushmen lieutenant (*Photo: Australian War Memorial*)

'I was on an observation post when we outspanned. I climbed a tree to get a better view and took a pair of glasses up the tree with me. I had a complete view of the country all around except as to one depression. Later on I saw Lt. Handcock and three troopers and one led horse issue from the depression. When Lt. Handcock came up I said, "I see you came in with a led horse and an empty saddle." He said, "Yes, we had a brush with the Boers. They ambushed us and killed one of our men." Then he added, "We beat them off and they were making for that kopje", indicating one by Hayes Farm. I thought at the time that it was most improbable that they could have passed without me seeing them from my observation post up the tree. I swear that I saw no Boers and no one else saw them. I do not believe there were any Boers present in the neighbourhood that day, certainly not in the direction indicated by Lt. Handcock for when we passed under the kopje they would certainly have opened fire whereas the facts are that one of our men, Trooper Churton, went right on top of the hill. I came to the conclusion that there had been foul play and that Lt. Handcock had himself shot Trooper Van Burens because he had spoken to the Dutch about the slaughter of the six.'

These six Boers were the ones for whose deaths Captain Taylor was charged. Despite this deposition and other testimony, none of it markedly different from that in the cases against the four BVC officers, Taylor and the two with him were acquitted, and the fact that those three were Englishmen rather than 'colonials' was later taken in Australia as being the only reason for their not being found guilty. Improbable as that sounds it was one of the factors which led to the ill-feeling engendered in Australia by this whole sorry affair. And then there was the shooting of the German missionary, the crime for which, popular feeling has it, Morant and Handcock were executed. Again I plead my own guilt in fostering this line of thought, partly for lack of anything substantive which said otherwise at the time I wrote my novel, partly because it made for a most effective dramatic ploy.

The thought that the Kaiser, seeking revenge for German honour, should have written to his cousin King Edward about it is an intriguing one, and I used it because it seemed to me then to be a possibility, and that word should then have passed from the King to Kitchener. It *still* seems to me to have been possible although I feel a much more probable sequence of events was that Kitchener, representing both the military and the government points of view, was anxious to perform three functions: to show the Boers Britain's desire to end the war and to prove this by openly damning any

Even more primitive than the humpy shown in the previous picture is this Boer shelter near Magersfontein (*Photo: Australian War Memorial*)

suggestion of British harshness towards Boers at large; to maintain the rigid standards of discipline and deportment he required of his soldiers; and to offset some of the condemnation of Britain in the foreign press. As a professional and very tough soldier he may well have condoned secretly the sorts of actions being carried on in areas like the Spelonken; he may even have suggested the 'no prisoners' approach and allowed the word to filter down unobtrusively through Colonel Hamilton and others, but he was hardly the type of man to issue a direct order of that kind which could so easily have drawn down fire on his own head.

With the death of a civilian (a German, and a man of the cloth at that) it was imperative that a public display of disapproval by the High Command should be made—and so the whole sorry mess had to come out. It should never be forgotten that, of all the charges, *this one of the murder of the missionary was one on which Morant and Handcock were found Not Guilty*. Had the pressure from above really been applied, had a perfect example of British justice been wanted for the international press, no better could have been found than to bring down a verdict of guilt for that one killing. Instead, the two men charged were acquitted on that count. The evidence just was not strong enough against them to prove that either or both murdered Daniel Heese of the Berlin Missionary Society.

How much do we know of what happened on that August day in 1901? The report of the trial in the press dealt with the evidence only briefly, probably because of the outcome. Had Morant and Handcock been found guilty it is likely that much more would have been said. It does, however, mention the account given by a native lad, Silas, and here, for the first time, is that account in full. It was sent with a covering note to Colonel Hall at Pietersburg by Reverend O. Krause of Kreuzberg.

'Sir,
I send Silas statement re Mr. Heese death what you have been asking me for the other day. I tried to repeat it in the same sentences Silas gave it to me, You may consider it to be a true translation of what Silas spoke to me in *his* language. Should you wish to have any explanation about the one or the other event reported in it, I will give same.

Yours Faithfully,
O. Krause.'

Pietersburg 9 September 1901.

'Silas reports:
I was in Spelonken and left there on the morning of the 23rd. in order to return home. Soon after midday I was overtaken at Mailaskop by Mr. Heese. He was sitting in his spider and reading a book. A while later it came to my mind that I could after all ask whether Mynheer would permit me to sit with him on his waggon in order to get home more quickly. The thought was followed by action and I ran after the waggon. Mr. Heese was already well ahead.

'While I was thus hurrying along, a rider came galloping behind me, going in the same direction. He wore khaki clothing such as the soldiers wear, a light-coloured hat with a cloth of motley colours (red, blue, white and black), and had stripes like a corporal. He was a young, stocky man; his face was shaved except for the moustache that he wore. He wore two cartridge-belts crossways over his shoulders and his breast pockets were filled with cartridges. His horse was of a bay colour, had a long tail and was not particularly well-conditioned. I greeted him and he replied with closed lips, "Mmm". From the back I recognised that the horse was shod.

'A while later I came to a spot from which one has an unhindered view to the next rise. It was there that the rider had dismounted, leading the horse by the bridle, had turned off into the bush. At the same time I noticed a waggon come down from the rise lying ahead of me. A little lower down in the hollow stood Mr. Heese's spider, unharnessed. When the waggon reached the spider, the owner (Van Rooyen) alighted and had a conversation, not very long, with Mr. Heese; then he took his leave and followed on foot after his waggon which had driven ahead. Van Rooyen was still walking on foot when I met him; he addressed me and asked me about "Where from?" and "Where to?" and whether the road towards Mailaskop was safe. I told him that I saw nothing and also that there was nothing to fear. Through this conversation I had lost a little time. Mr. Heese had in the meantime harnessed up and drove on up the rise. I hurried after him and had come within a distance of about 300 yards from the spider (the distances were measured off later) but could not see the vehicle on account of a bend in the road, when a shot was fired, immediately afterwards a second, a third, a fourth.

'I asked myself what that might mean, but did not think anything bad. In the period from the first to the fourth shot I had only progressed 16 yards because I had slowed down my steps; however since I could hear nothing further I went on, always on the lookout whether I would discover something. Then I see to the right of the road a vehicle—the spider of Mr. Heese—standing, the pole however not in the direction of Pietersburg, but turned around towards Spelonken, from where he had come. I did not see the mules in front of the spider; the grass indeed was rather long (3 to 5 feet high) nevertheless I would have had to see the animals. They were not there. Behind the spider stood a horse, bridled and saddled, with the reins lying on it; and the horse was the same one that I had seen shortly before, the bay horse of the rider who, galloping past me, had overtaken me this side of Mailaskop.

'The spider stood only about 50 yards off the side of the road but I could see neither anyone in the spider nor anyone in the vicinity of it. But the inkling rose up in me that the shots, the empty waggon and the saddled horse had to have a sinister connection; and fear crept into my soul. While I moved hesitatingly forward with my eyes turned sideways and took little notice of the road I caught sight of the lifeless body of a Coloured. I was so scared that I cried out loudly: What is that?—here a person has been murdered—who has murdered him? And I recognised this dead person. I recognised his face and recognised his clothing; I had seen him at Elim and seen him near Mailaskop when the spider drove past—it was Mr. Heese's driver. A gunshot in the forehead had torn away the scalp and brains came forth. I laid my hand on the body and felt that it was quite warm. Such a terror came over me that I could think of nothing else than to run home and report.'

That is as close to any eyewitness account as we are ever likely to get, and it really helps very little. Silas calls the mysterious rider's horse a bay; the witnesses in court spoke of a chestnut; both colours could be called brown—and the press report used just that word. Silas's description of the rider as young, stocky, and moustached could apply to Handcock—but not the mention of the corporal's stripes, unless it *was* Handcock in someone else's jacket. Most effective of all in court was the evidence of Mrs Schiels and Mrs Bristow, each of whom corroborated Handcock's story that he was with them in turn, something like sixty-five kilometres away from the scene of the shooting.

A week before that report was sent in Colonel Hall sent *his* report of the affair to Mr Krause and there is an odd emphasis about it. He says first that Captain Taylor warned the missionary that the road was unsafe and advised him to wait and that Morant repeated the warning and also suggested that Mr Heese wait for a patrol to accompany him. Then he writes of the finding of the body. 'The party went to Bandolierskopjes and about 3/4 mile on the north side of it they found a trap and nearer the Kopje a body. On it were passes issued to the Revd. Heese. There were bullet wounds in the left breast and left hand. The body was covered up with two rugs. There were traces of 5 horses which had evidently been tied up to the trap for some time. The horses' tracks led to the Zoutspansberg mountains.'

This seems to be the only reference anywhere to the tracks of these five horses; the lad Silas made no mention of them, but then he was in a panic when he ran off. The patrol which found the body — several days after the killing — was led by Handcock, so the presumption is that he gave the information to Colonel Hall.

It is not possible to ignore two possibilities in this context. One is that a Boer group had found Heese's body before the patrol arrived, which would account for the tracks of the five horses but it seems to me that if Boers had found the corpse they would either have taken it in to a mission or a property, or given it decent burial on the spot and passed the word on. The other possibility is that Handcock was simply inventing the tracks to cover himself or someone else. Since in the courtroom so much weight clearly attached to the evidence of the two women, Mrs Schiels and Mrs Bristow, that Handcock was with them on the fatal day, it has to be considered that theirs was possibly false testimony. If they were telling the truth Handcock was patently innocent; if they were lying the circumstantial evidence points strongly to Handcock's guilt.

There is only one other thing worth pointing out about this case. More than a quarter of a century after it all happened George Witton wrote to J. F. Thomas. His letter was held by the Mitchell Library in Sydney and was not available for general viewing until 1970. In that letter, written in October 1929, Witton says: 'Personally I think the attitude you take with regard to Morant and Handcock and the Hesse case is not the right one. I am inclined to think that neither of them took you into their confidence over that case. Up to the time of the Court of Inquiry when I was charged with complicity in his death I had no more knowledge of how Hesse came by his death than the babe unborn nor did I have at any time the slightest suspicion that Morant or Handcock was connected with it. It staggered me at the time but my statement in reply I think cleared me of that count at that inquiry. Subsequently when we were allowed to see each other Morant told me that Handcock had broken down and confessed to everything including shooting Hesse. I saw Handcock shortly afterwards and asked him about the Hesse business. He said, "Why weren't you standing beside Morant when he asked me if I was game to follow the Missionary and wipe him out?"

'I had been with them up to the time Morant returned from interviewing Hesse when he drove past the fort. I left them then and

113

went to my tent and did not see them again until they came in to dinner about 7 o'clock. I believe Morant got Handcock to deny the previous statement in which he had made "*a clean breast of everything*" and they got to work to frame up an alabi [*sic*] which you know was successful and the means of their acquittal.'

The Court of Inquiry and the courts martial did something more than examine, try, and find verdicts. They succeeded in bringing out some fairly unsavoury facts about the conduct of British troops in the field and the attitudes of some of their commanders. The witnesses brought for the defence by Thomas showed enough times that similar sorts of action to those for which men were being tried had taken place, on a number of occasions and in a number of places, and that officers up to field rank at least had condoned them—in some cases had incited them. Even the limited reports which came out of the courtroom, and all of them after the fact, made it plain to the British public that the Boers alone could not be accused of breaking the usages of war. But by then it was too late for it to help the four men in the dock.

The Heese case went before the court on 17 February 1902. Five days later the Under-Secretary for War, St John Brodrick, wrote a private letter to Kitchener. It began:

'My Dear Lord Kitchener,
Your report on the Court Martial on Bush Veldt Carbiniers came to hand last night. It is a most deplorable performance and, if it gets out, as I fear it will, even the strong measures we are taking will not undo the disgrace it inflicts on our Colonial Forces. I should myself have been inclined to shoot all these officers—but you are in the best position to judge and I am agreeing with you.'

The accused men were in breach of Military Law and were tried by courts martial, which means that their judges were soldiers and almost certainly not versed in the intricacies of any form of legal argument beyond the most straightforward. But it must be remembered that they had the assistance and advice of the Judge-Advocate-General's Department, of men skilled in interpretation of the law. For the accused to have been passed on by the Court of Inquiry to a court martial it must have been felt, legally as well as militarily, that there was adequate cause to bring major charges against them.

Here are some extracts from the Judge-Advocate-General's

Minute Book in Pretoria in which aspects of the Court of Inquiry are commented on: 'As to Lieut. Picton B.V.C. he appears to have been accessory to murder equally with the other members of the so-called Court Martial and may I think be charged with the capital offence.'

'The idea that no prisoners were to be taken in the Spelonken appears to have been started by the late Captain Hunt and after his death continued by orders given personally by Captain Taylor. The statement that Captain Hunt's body had been maltreated is in no way corroborated and the reprisals undertaken by Lt. Morant on this idea were utterly unjustifiable.'

'Lieut. Witton acquiesced with illegal executions of the wounded Boer Visser and took a personal part in the massacre of the 8 surrendered Boers on 23rd August.'

The Minute Book goes on to record the J-A-G's remarks about a number of points of procedure and evidence, in almost every case soberly finding the outcome to be justified, the accused to have been rightly tried, the sentences to have been fairly awarded. In *almost* every case—there are two exceptions. In the case of the wanton murder of six Boers the remarks are: '. . . I think taking all the circumstances of the case into consideration the responsibility should rest with the Officer, Captain Taylor, who gave the order . . .' and, on a later page: '(I forward) also the record of a Military Court held under Martial Law for the trial of Alfred Taylor, an Intelligence Agent. The latter was not tried by a Court Martial under the Army Act as at date of trial he had ceased to be subject to Military Law for more than 3 months.'

The conjunction of Martial Law and Military Law and Taylor's sliding between them may have satisfied bureaucracy but nonetheless leaves a sick taste on the tongue. The other exception to the general tone of agreement by the J-A-G was not, in any case, helpful to the prisoners: 'According to rules of Procedure 48 and 67 the trial on the separate charge sheets should have proceeded up to and including the Findings—but one sentence should have been awarded each prisoner for all the offences of which he was convicted. This irregularity has not in my opinion inflicted any injustice on Lieut. Morant but I am not prepared to say that it has not done so in the other 3 cases. A heap of irrelevant evidence was admitted by the Court on the part of the defence despite the ruling of the Judge-Advocate who I consider was justified in protesting.'

One final excerpt from that long-hidden Minute Book, referring to the method criticised above: 'It resulted from this mode of procedure that Lieut. Morant has been convicted three different times of murder and sentenced three times to Death.

Infantrymen of the British Army in Pretoria, Kruger's lost capital (*Photo: Australian War Memorial*)

'Lieuts. Picton, Handcock and Whitton [*sic*] have been convicted once of manslaughter and sentenced to cashiering; Lieut. Handcock has been also twice convicted of murder and sentenced to Death twice.

'Lieut. Whitton has been also once convicted of Murder and sentenced to Death.

'From the above it appears that the responsibility for these illegal acts were in the following order: 1. Morant. 2. Handcock. 3. Whitton. 4. Picton.'

And so it was. Taylor escaped it all. Lenehan was reprimanded. Picton was cashiered. Witton's sentence of death was commuted to one of life imprisonment. Morant and Handcock were shot.

5

Consequences

The trials were over; the cases were closed. From the late afternoon of 17 February 1902 until dinner three days later the prisoners were held in separate cells, able to meet for a short spell each afternoon and for an evening meal, able then to discuss what might happen to them. Witton has it that Harry Morant was in a depressed mood (hardly surprising!), and surely it must have been a bitterly tense time for them all. The feeling lightened more than a little on the evening of 20 February when all that was left of the BVC met for dinner—the four prisoners and Lenehan, together with Thomas and Taylor. There was a visitor to raise their spirits during that meal, an orderly sent in to say that a Staff officer had said in the Brigade office that all the accused men had been exonerated. But it was a short-lived happiness.

Early the next morning the men were taken to Pietersburg Railway Station in irons. Among the documents recently discovered in South Africa is the Army Headquarters order for their move to Pretoria.

Again according to Witton the brave, almost brash, Harry Morant, when the handcuffs were locked on to his wrists, broke down completely and wept. The party was escorted by a guard with fixed bayonets and locked into two armoured rail trucks—Witton with Lenehan, and Morant, Picton, and Handcock together. The army was taking no chances. The train reached Pretoria on 21 February and Lenehan was separated there. The others were taken to Pretoria Gaol where they were stripped, searched, and medically examined before having their own clothes returned to them. They were still in uniform, still wearing their badges of rank, and it seems strange and demeaning—to the uniform as well as to the men—that they should have been taken in irons and under armed guard through the streets of two cities.

PRESSING & CONFIDENTIAL.   A.H.Q./828/32/B.

Army Head Quarters,
Pretoria, 21st February, 1902.

Provost Marshal,
    A r m y.

    The following telegram has been despatched to the O.C., L. of C., North, Pietersburg :-

    "February 18th. A 9525 Send prisoners Major Lenehan, Lieutenants Morant, Picton, Handcock and Witton, to Pretoria under an adequate escort commanded by a competent officer. They are all to be handcuffed except Major Lenehan. Every precaution must be taken against possibility of escape. Report departure to this office and G.O.C., Pretoria, giving name of officer commanding. Acknowledge".

    The G.O.C., Pretoria, has been instructed to have the prisoners and escort met on arrival and to arrange for the safe custody of the former in Pretoria.

    The finding and sentence of the Court in the case of Major Lenehan will be promulgated as soon as practicable after his arrival and he is then to be despatched to Cape Town and embarked for Australia as quickly as possible. Will you be so good as to take steps to have him carefully supervised until he actually sails.

                          R. Whigham, Major,

A photostat copy of the order instructing that the prisoners be transferred in handcuffs

On the morning of 23 February they were moved to the condemned cells where, oddly, they were given more liberty than they had had for weeks; they were permitted to have their cell doors open from early morning to early evening and were allowed to enjoy the small luxuries that many people were sending in to them.

They still had no idea of what was going to happen to them and most of a week dragged by before they found out. On Thursday 26 February they were called in turn into the Governor's office, Morant first, then Handcock, Witton, and Picton. Two sentences of death, one of death commuted to life imprisonment, one of cashiering. The verdicts were like a series of hammer-blows and for the two who were to die there was the sure knowledge that life was suddenly a matter of short hours only.

There is no established law, act, or order which sets out the manner in which a firing-squad should proceed about its grisly task. In the British Army of that time, and into the Great War, it was a matter of orders being passed downwards, an inexorable progression which began as soon as the sentence of death was confirmed. In this case, once Kitchener had signed the paper his headquarters at once ordered the next formation down the ladder to deal with it and, while the HQ signals staff was transmitting the order down the line, the two men most affected by it were back in their cells, also writing.

Morant wrote directly to Kitchener seeking a reprieve; Handcock also wrote to the Commander-in-Chief asking that the Australian Government care for his children. Witton sent urgent telegrams to a friend at Cape Town and to his brother in Australia. Thomas, meanwhile, tried to see Kitchener in the hope of an appeal to the King. But Kitchener was 'away from headquarters' for a few days on 'a tour of inspection' and was 'out of touch', which seems a little strange for a Commander-in-Chief in time of war — and Thomas was told that in any case the sentences had already been approved in England. St John Brodrick's letter to Kitchener leaves little doubt of that, though no one knows whether, in fact, King Edward was approached with anything other than advice on the matter. Morant's petition was answered with the same news of Kitchener's absence; Handcock's was returned to him unanswered, and neither of Witton's telegrams was delivered.

By the time the men knew all that, by the evening of that day, Division had sent an order down to Brigade where the necessary paperwork was quickly done and signed and forwarded.

A pleasant dinner was sent in to the gaol that evening and the four prisoners were allowed to share it in Witton's cell, Morant remarking that it was 'The Last Supper' for them. He and Handcock were

Reg. No.	Name	1902. General Description			
		Sex	Age	Race	Occupation
309	Harry Harboard Morant	Male	35	English	Army Officer (Lieut.)
310	Peter Joseph Handcock	Male	34	Australian	Army Officer

Description H.B. Morant: Eyes – Grey, Nose – Prominent,

Description P.J. Handcock: Eyes – Blue, Nose – prominent,

A photostat copy of the page of the prison record book showing the entries for prisoners 309 and 310

Receipt in Prison			Crime	Date of trial	Sentence	Discharged	
Date		What Authority				Date	Cause
22 February		H. W. Hutson Asst. Provost Marshall				27 February 1902	Shot
22 February		H W Hutson A. P. M.				27 February 1902	Shot
		— Brown, Height — 5 ft 6¾ in			Trace marks left arm.		
		— light Brown, Height — 5 ft 10½ in			Trace marks left arm Birthmark left eye scars from scald side of back & shoulder back mottled.		

permitted to spend that night in one cell and it was from the barred trap in the door of that grim little room that they said their goodbyes to Witton and Picton very early the next morning, Witton being taken off for transportation to a life sentence in a British prison and Picton on his way out of the country as a disgraced officer.

On that last evening, during the shared meal, the order-signals were moving from Brigade to regimental level, to the Commanding Officer of the Cameron Highlanders, telling him to make all the necessary arrangements for a firing-squad. Regimental routine dictated the procedure from then on — the task would fall to the Duty Platoon and its Platoon Officer. The Regimental Sergeant-Major met the Regimental Quartermaster-Sergeant at his Store where twelve rifles were drawn from the racks, checked, and loaded by the two Warrant Officers, eleven with ball ammunition, one with a blank round. The Duty Platoon was paraded and the first three files of four men were told off to report to the Quartermaster's Store. There they were issued with the rifles, loaded and with their safety-catches on, none of the men knowing which rifle was loaded with a blank. They were at once paraded before the officer commanding the Duty Platoon, inspected and, with their sergeant, were marched away to the flat piece of ground behind the gaol. As a Base unit they were in khaki tunics and kilts, the tartan not covered by the khaki aprons worn by many Highland regiments in the field, and the first true light of the day would have been bright on their gaiters and the red-and-white checkered tops folded over them. They were halted, turned, and formed into a single file. The order was given, 'For inspection, port arms' and the rifles were held steady across the men's chests, muzzles pointing up over the left shoulders, bolts worked and held open so that the Platoon Sergeant could move along the line checking to see the round of .303 ammunition lying ready in the breech. When the bolts were locked home, those rounds were ready to be fired. Then the squad was brought to attention and held there, only their eyes moving to watch as Harry Morant and Peter Handcock were marched out on their last parade.

It was six o'clock on the morning of 27 February 1902, and there were about thirty onlookers, some of them troopers and NCOs of the Bush Veldt Carbineers.

The record of those last hours, as Prisoners No. 309 and 310, end in the column marked 'Discharged'. Under 'Cause' there is the single word 'Shot'.

George Witton tells in his book how, during the wait at Pretoria Railway Station, he distinctly heard 'in the clear morning air the report of the volley of the firing party, the death-knell of my late comrades . . . so went out two brave and fearless soldiers, men that the Empire could ill afford to lose.'

In the empty cell there were some things which the two men had left behind. One was a letter from Handcock to his sister, Mrs Dempsey, written on 27 February:

'Dear Sister,

I have but an hour or so longer to exist and altho my brain has been harrised for four long weary months I cant refrain from writing you a few last lines, I am going to find out the grand secret, I will face my God, with the firm belief I am innocent of murder. I obeyed my orders and served my King as I thought best. If I over steped my duty I can only ask my People and country for forgiveness. Tell poor Polly to take care of little Illem for me at all costs. They were my greatist comforts at Home & my greatest trouble now I hope my country will see my children cared for I will die brave for the sake of all, God, forgive any enemys & give you peace for ever I have not heard if our Brother Eugene was killed in this retched war or not But if not tell him & Will I have gone to rest Tell Peter and Willie to be good to their sister, God, be with you in your trouble.

from your fond Brother
    P. J. Handcock.
Australia for ever
   Amen.'

It seems strange that in those fading hours before dawn he should have written to a sister, not to his wife. Indeed, Mrs Handcock knew nothing of the affair until well after it was all over. Here is part of a report from the Bathurst newspaper, the *National Advocate*, dated 29 March 1902: 'When the information was first read locally in the newspapers, there were very few who suspected that Lieutenant P. J. Handcock given as from West Australia, was identical with the man of the same name who had resided in Bathurst. However, there was a returned soldier in Bathurst who knew Lieutenant P. J. Handcock well and the force he was with, and so soon as this soldier read of the occurrence in the Sydney papers and saw the names of the officers he knew at once that the wife of one of them was no other than the lady with whom he was lodging. He immediately placed the paper away out of sight, and when Mr. Maurice Clines, cousin of Mrs. Handcock, came home to tea on Wednesday night he communicated the extraordinary and sad news to him, and later on the intelligence was communicated to Mrs. Handcock. She was greatly concerned and could scarcely credit that her husband had been dead so long without her knowing it. When a representative of this paper called

australians then we will send you the Poto of the Grav the Dies as Brave as Men could saying Good By to each other. Everyone that looked on said it was A shame to shoot 2 so Brave men I Hope you will for his mates sake an your Brothers do your Best for the children his Person Belongings will Reach you Later on when the are Given out from the Prison you will get several letters from friends here Mostly from Cangroo Land. I must Draw to A close this time By saying good By God Bless you all from your *sincire* friend.

J. H. Morrow
Warder Pretoria
Gaol
Transvall'

One other thing. I have a scrap of paper torn from a notepad and I believe it is the last thing Peter Handcock ever wrote. It is addressed on the reverse to Mrs Dempsey and there is a note written cornerwise near that in someone else's hand saying 'Horse of Handcock he wishes to go to Dr. Leonard, Pietersburg'. The ragged piece of paper is before me as I write this, and looking at it it is easy to visualise the scene in the cell on that still, cool night, a lantern on the table between the two men, their small possessions sorted.

I conjecture Morant was keeping up a brave enough front and Handcock, always loyal, would surely have followed the man he had followed in so much else that was desperate. He wrote boldly with a soft pencil, '*Australia For Ever*. May her Sons Never Fail. P. J. Handcock'. And I see him a little later, reaching across to pick up a pencil again, a darker one, perhaps the one Morant had been using. And he wrote firmly, 'The only request is to let my People know I die with the belief I am innocent of murder'.

He was to sign his name once more in those final hours. There is a photograph which has been published frequently and which shows a group of men seated outside a tent — Handcock, Morant, a man who may have been Dr Johnston or Dr Neel, Hunt, Taylor, and Picton. I have the original of that photograph. Written in pencil on the back of it are these words —

'To the Reverend Canon Fisher, Pretoria.
The night before we're shot.
We shot the Boers who killed and mutilated *our* friend (the best mate I had on Earth)

Harry Harbord Morant
Peter Joseph Handcock'

comrades . . . so went out two brave and fearless soldiers, men that the Empire could ill afford to lose.'

In the empty cell there were some things which the two men had left behind. One was a letter from Handcock to his sister, Mrs Dempsey, written on 27 February:

'Dear Sister,

I have but an hour or so longer to exist and altho my brain has been harrised for four long weary months I cant refrain from writing you a few last lines, I am going to find out the grand secret, I will face my God, with the firm belief I am innocent of murder. I obeyed my orders and served my King as I thought best. If I over steped my duty I can only ask my People and country for forgiveness. Tell poor Polly to take care of little Illem for me at all costs. They were my greatist comforts at Home & my greatest trouble now I hope my country will see my children cared for I will die brave for the sake of all, God, forgive any enemys & give you peace for ever I have not heard if our Brother Eugene was killed in this retched war or not But if not tell him & Will I have gone to rest Tell Peter and Willie to be good to their sister, God, be with you in your trouble.

    from your fond Brother
          P. J. Handcock.

Australia for ever
    Amen.'

It seems strange that in those fading hours before dawn he should have written to a sister, not to his wife. Indeed, Mrs Handcock knew nothing of the affair until well after it was all over. Here is part of a report from the Bathurst newspaper, the *National Advocate*, dated 29 March 1902: 'When the information was first read locally in the newspapers, there were very few who suspected that Lieutenant P. J. Handcock given as from West Australia, was identical with the man of the same name who had resided in Bathurst. However, there was a returned soldier in Bathurst who knew Lieutenant P. J. Handcock well and the force he was with, and so soon as this soldier read of the occurrence in the Sydney papers and saw the names of the officers he knew at once that the wife of one of them was no other than the lady with whom he was lodging. He immediately placed the paper away out of sight, and when Mr. Maurice Clines, cousin of Mrs. Handcock, came home to tea on Wednesday night he communicated the extraordinary and sad news to him, and later on the intelligence was communicated to Mrs. Handcock. She was greatly concerned and could scarcely credit that her husband had been dead so long without her knowing it. When a representative of this paper called on Mrs. Handcock she was found to be in great grief, having become resigned to the fact that the news must only be all too true. She had received many letters from him, the last being about three months ago. "Were you not anxious as to your husband's safety when you did not hear from him for three months?" interrogated the reporter of the *National Advocate*. "No, I was not. He spoke in his last letter of going to England to see his father's relations . . . consequently I thought he was on his way to England and was expecting to hear from him any day." "What about your family?" queried the pressman. Here Mrs. Handcock, who was visibly affected throughout, was not slow in expressing her feelings as to the treatment she had received. "Would you think that the British authorities would treat a widow and three children as I have been treated? My husband has been dead a month, and not one of us has been acquainted of it. I've heard of the cruelty of the Boers spoken of, but could anything be more cruel than this treatment?"'

A while later Peter Handcock's widow married her cousin and became Mrs Clines.

There was another letter, written by a warder in Pretoria Gaol on the day after the execution. The spelling has been left exactly as it is in the original.

'Dear Mrs. Dempsey

I Hope you will Excuse Me for taking the Liberty of writing to you it is with regret I have to Do so I was the last warder on Duty over your Brother *an my* friend. A *South Australia* H. H. Morant was out here over 2 years in the South Australian Mt Rifles an served trough the war Got the *Bar* for 'Cape' Colony and A *Bar* for Johannesburg an A Bar for Pretoria also the Bar for *Belfast* Medal also I was his Greatest friend all trough an got the same Honors But the troops went home over 12 months ago an Morant went on as Lieut in the Bush velth Carboniers an I went on as Guard on the Railway an only Got Transfered to Pretoria Prison A few weeks as *warder* an on the 22 your Brother an Morant an 2 more *Lieutenants* 1 Victorian an one from Newzeland 4 in all 2 sentensed Penelservitude an the other 2 shot the fased Death without A Murmur an *had* only 48 hours notice of the fact your Brothers trouble Was you an his *children* the faced Death 'as' *Brave* as men could an I was with them until the last the shot 30 odd Boars on Acount of the Boars shooting there Captain the say the are not Guilty of the charge the were sentensed to Death for shooting there mates it was as nice a fonerl as Ever Left the Gaol there was no less than 20 officers an A Number of australians followed the Remains there will Be A Head Stone Erected By

Above: A photograph showing the main cast in the Breaker Morant saga. From left: Handcock, Morant, either Dr Johnston or Dr Neel, Hunt, Taylor, and Picton. *Below:* The confession in pencil on the back of the previous photograph, obviously written by Morant but also signed by Handcock (*Photo: Author's collection*)

australians then we will send you the Poto of the Grav the Dies as Brave as Men could saying Good By to each other. Everyone that looked on said it was A shame to shoot 2 so Brave men I Hope you will for his mates sake an your Brothers do your Best for the children his Person Belongings will Reach you Later on when the are Given out from the Prison you will get several letters from friends here Mostly from Cangroo Land. I must Draw to A close this time By saying good By God Bless you all from your *sincire* friend.

J. H. Morrow
Warder Pretoria
Gaol
Transvall'

One other thing. I have a scrap of paper torn from a notepad and I believe it is the last thing Peter Handcock ever wrote. It is addressed on the reverse to Mrs Dempsey and there is a note written cornerwise near that in someone else's hand saying 'Horse of Handcock he wishes to go to Dr. Leonard, Pietersburg'. The ragged piece of paper is before me as I write this, and looking at it it is easy to visualise the scene in the cell on that still, cool night, a lantern on the table between the two men, their small possessions sorted.

I conjecture Morant was keeping up a brave enough front and Handcock, always loyal, would surely have followed the man he had followed in so much else that was desperate. He wrote boldly with a soft pencil, '*Australia For Ever*. May her Sons Never Fail. P. J. Handcock'. And I see him a little later, reaching across to pick up a pencil again, a darker one, perhaps the one Morant had been using. And he wrote firmly, 'The only request is to let my People know I die with the belief I am innocent of murder'.

He was to sign his name once more in those final hours. There is a photograph which has been published frequently and which shows a group of men seated outside a tent—Handcock, Morant, a man who may have been Dr Johnston or Dr Neel, Hunt, Taylor, and Picton. I have the original of that photograph. Written in pencil on the back of it are these words—

'To the Reverend Canon Fisher, Pretoria.
The night before we're shot.
We shot the Boers who killed and mutilated *our* friend (the best mate I had on Earth)

Harry Harbord Morant
Peter Joseph Handcock'

With all the argument, all the controversy, about the actions of these two and about their execution, I suppose there is something fitting in the thought that even the disposal of their personal effects led to dispute. Long-concealed in archival records in Pretoria was this exchange of correspondence.

'From, President to
Committee of Adjustment, A.P.M. Pretoria Dist.
Would you kindly cause the effects of the late Lieuts. Handcock and Morant to be handed over to the N.C.O. of this message
Sgt. Smith R.Bde.   Sgd. J. R. Longley, Capt.
14/3/02   President of Committee of Adjust.'

'To Director of Prisoners, Pretoria.
Please hand over these effects to Capt. Longley's representative.
                       Sgd. H. D. Hutson, Captain.
17/3/02   A.P.M. Pretoria Dist.'

'Private effects of late Lieut. Morant was sent to Pietersburg to C. W. Surgeon Johnston. Late Lieut. Handcock's were handed to A.P.M. Pretoria District.
Receipt for same in my possession.
                       Sgd. J. Barratt, Gaoler.'

'To A.P.M. Pretoria.
Forwarded in continuation of my memo of yesterday. Please see gaolers remarks. Will you kindly inform me of the authority under which the late Lt. Morant's kit was handed over to Dr. Johnston. The orders that the committee received, were that these officers effects were to be sold, and the sum realised together with any pay due, after settling just claims was to be credited to the War Office. Return requested.
                       Sgd. J. R. Longley, Capt.
19/3/02   President, Com. of Adjust.'

'Director of Prisons.
Please see Minute 4.
19/3/02   Sgd. H. D. Hutson, Capt.'

'The Provost Marshal, A.H.Qrs.
The kit of the late Lieut. Morant was sent by my orders to Dr. Johnston, Civil Surgeon, Pietersburg, who was appointed Executor by the Will of the deceased Officer.

It is regretted that the wishes of the Military Authorities were not communicated to me in this matter, and it is obvious that, under the circumstances, the private property of prisoners who have been removed or executed, cannot be stored for an indefinite period in the gaol.

Sgd. J. Garland,
Director of Prisons.'

20th. March 1902.

We do not know what Dr Johnston did with Morant's personal things but something more than twenty years ago a clergyman called West wrote to the *Bulletin* saying that he had been commissioned by the War Office in 1902 to take some possessions of Morant's to his family at Fordingbridge in Hampshire. And the daughter of the Bloemfontein Provost Marshal had another piece to add to this tattered tapestry. Her father had been told off to act as an alternative prosecutor at the courts martial, but he was sympathetic to Morant as a man and they became friendly. According to the daughter, Miss Bolton, Morant had given her father his watch, the picture of a girl, and a notebook and asked for them to be taken to his mother, together with a letter he had written to her. These things were sent to England where the Provost Marshal's wife and daughter took them into Hampshire, to what was called 'a lovely old country house'. They were welcomed by a pretty, white-haired woman called Mrs Morant who had tears running down her cheeks when she said goodbye to them.

All of which leads towards the belief that Morant was, indeed, a son of the Morants, legitimate or otherwise—except for one thing: the Provost Marshal's daughter referred to the woman as 'Mrs Morant'; Admiral George Digby Morant had been knighted by then and his wife would have been Lady Morant.

The Hampshire County Archivist, in a letter in June 1981, had a definite word to say:

'... I have been in correspondence with the Morant family of South West Hampshire. The family certainly had and still have a "goodly" house in Hampshire. They also know all about "Breaker Morant", and it is clear that The Breaker was an imposter and had nothing to do with the Hampshire family. The member of the family with whom I have been in correspondence tells me that a South African Hotel sent an unpaid bill of Breaker Morant's during the Boer War to his (my correspondent's) grandmother. A family conference was held to see if anyone knew anything of him, but no one did. The family do not wish to appear to have anything to hide—they simply do not know who "The Breaker" was ...'

So the mystery persists. By seven in the morning of 27 February 1902 Morant and Handcock were dead. The other lives went on.

HARRY PICTON

He remains as unknown after the events as he was before, a shade of a man with an indistinct past who vanished into limbo. When he said goodbye to the two men in the condemned cell he was taken out of Pretoria Gaol a disgraced and deprived man. As a cashiered officer he was not entitled to any of the decorations he had been awarded and he had been stripped of his Distinguished Conduct Medal and his South Africa Medal with its six campaign clasps. He was to be removed to England by whatever speedy means were available and the brief exchanges of official correspondence offer almost all the information there has been about him since then.

From Army Headquarters on 25 February 1902: 'I have sent you official instructions that *Picton* is to be removed and embarked for England as soon as possible after promulgation of sentence'.

On that same day, from the Deputy Assistant Adjutant-General's office and marked 'Confidential and Pressing': 'Will you please arrange that Lieut. Picton B.V.C. who has been sentenced to be "cashiered" is despatched to Cape Town as quickly as possible after the promulgation of the sentence and embarked for England. He should be supervised until he actually sails'.

A telegram from the G.O.C., Cape Town, to the Provost Marshal at Pretoria on 27 February: 'Departure will be reported in due course'.

Almost a fortnight later, on 12 March, there was a follow-up to that telegram — 'Picton left for Canada on 10th. inst.' (Witton was on the same ship, from the Cape to Canada, to Queenstown in Ireland, and then on to England.)

On 30 March the Assistant Provost Marshal at Army HQ wrote to his counterpart at Pietersburg: 'Can you please furnish me with the address of Lieut. Picton, late B.V.C. so that O.C. 1st. Wilts. Regt. may recover money due for mess accounts.'

The answer, next day, was brusque: 'I do not know it. S.O. Overseas Forces might as I fancy he was at one time a member of an Australian Contingent.'

The query was sent to the Senior Officer, Overseas Forces, who simply passed the buck on, saying 'I have no knowledge of Picton's whereabouts' and, on 14 April, Lt.-Colonel Poore, the Provost Marshal at Army HQ, wrote to the Chief Paymaster in Pretoria: 'This man was cashiered and sent Home to England. I think you have some money belonging to him to meet such cases as these. Can you deal with this case please?'

On 17 April the Station Paymaster wrote back: 'A cheque for £11.9.9 on a/c of mess bill H. Picton was forwarded by me to President Mess Committee 2nd. Wilts. Regt. on 4th inst.'

In view of that correspondence it seems possible that Picton's mess bill with the 1st. Wiltshires was actually paid into the account of the 2nd. Wiltshires! At all events, as far as the Army was concerned, the Picton problem was over. As far as the world at large was concerned, he just disappeared.

According to Witton, he made a fiery statement when he landed in England, denying a pro-Boer version of the case which had appeared in an Irish newspaper. The next (and only other) thing we know about him came in Witton's letter to Thomas twenty-seven years later. 'I have very little knowledge of any BVC officers. The last I heard of Picton was shortly after my return to Australia. He was then riding racehorses on the Continent.'

And he rode right out of our ken.

GEORGE WITTON

In the case of the killing of the eight Boers, the findings were these:

The court sentence the prisoners —	Sentence
Lieut. H. H. Morant, Bushveldt Carbineers, to suffer death by being shot.	Death
Lieut. P. J. Handcock, Bushveldt Carbineers, to suffer death by being shot.	Death
Lieut. G. R. Witton, Bushveldt Carbineers, to suffer death by being shot.	Death

Signed at Pietersburg, this 4th. day of February, 1902.

                                                    H. C. DENNY, Lt.-Col.
C. S. COPLAND, Major,   President.
Judge-Advocate.

RECOMMENDATION TO MERCY

The court recommend Lieut. H. H. Morant to mercy on the following grounds: —

Provocation received by the maltreatment of the body of his intimate friend, Capt. Hunt.

Want of previous military experience and complete ignorance of military law and military procedure.

His good service throughout the war.

The court recommend Lieut. P. J. Handcock and Lieut. G. R. Witton to mercy on the following grounds:—
1. The court consider both were influenced by Lieut. Morant's orders, and thought they were doing their duty in obeying them.
2. Their complete ignorance of military law and custom.
3. Their good services throughout the war.

H. C. DENNY, Lt.-Col.
President.

I confirm the finding and sentence in the case of Lieuts. Morant and Handcock.
I confirm the finding in the case of Lieut. Witton, but commute the sentence to one of penal servitude for life.
25th February, 1902.   KITCHENER, General.

On that same day the Provost Marshal at Army Headquarters received an instruction from the Deputy Assistant Adjutant-General.

'The sentence of Death passed by a General Court-Martial upon Lieutenants Morant and Handcock has been confirmed by the General Commanding-in-Chief, and the G.O.C., Pretoria District, has been instructed to arrange that the sentence is carried out within the precincts of the Gaol at 6 a.m. on Thursday, 27th instant. The sentence in the case of Witton has been commuted to Penal Servitude for Life and he is to be despatched to Cape Town for transfer to the United Kingdom in the ordinary manner.'

That 'ordinary manner' began with handcuffs and an armed escort, bayonets fixed. There was the rushed and muted farewell to companions and the train to Cape Town where, in the Castle Military Prison, Witton found Lenehan being securely held until he could be embarked for Australia. The cell at the castle was all there was of home for Witton until the second week of March, his first taste of the years to come, and he filled the time writing letters and cables, all of which he claims were suppressed. The guard on him was strict and Baudinet, previously a BVC officer, was refused permission to visit him.

Life as a prisoner became easier aboard the *Canada*. There was a small cabin built into the shipboard guardroom area and this was Witton's; Picton was also aboard and able to move without restraint—he was, of course, a civilian again—and with his help and that of the O.C. Troops and a reasonable police sergeant, Witton was able to spend his time above decks, get his meals from the saloon, and even be allotted a batman.

The arrival in England changed all that.

There were a number of military prisoners on board and they, with Witton, were labelled and handcuffed and taken off by escort, Witton cuffed to a young Lieutenant. Then it was through the night to Gosport Military Prison and the introduction to true prison life.

Gosport was bread and water and gruel and picking oakum (rubbing bristly rope to separate the strands) and Witton's account of it, and of prison life in general, has a strangely Dickensian ring about it.

Towards the end of April 1902 he was moved to Lewes Gaol, in khaki stripped of insignia, in manacles and leg irons, and into a prison where the slightly better food was offset by the cropping of his hair near to the bone. There, at least he found a friendly chaplain and was given access to some books and magazines, but the bulk of his time was spent in the endless dreariness of sewing drab canvas clothing. He had begun attempts at petitioning the authorities almost at once but met with a blank wall of refusal and rejection from the War Office, and his constant requests to interview prison visitors did him little good. His health was suffering—which is hardly surprising when you consider he had had almost two years of hard campaigning in South Africa, then the mental turmoil of the trials and the shock of the sentence.

There was another move, to Portland Prison where his cell was only a metre wide and two metres high and long, furnished with a canvas hammock, a tiny drop-table, and a wooden stool—and where he expected to have to spend the rest of his life. He was put to work in the foundry and tinsmithing shop, in an atmosphere heavy with the fumes of acids and the heat of the furnace; a bad contrast to the small, chill cell and the stink of 200 prisoners in close proximity.

His sickness grew worse and he was, at last, taken into the prison hospital where it was confirmed that he was suffering from typhoid fever. For more than two months he was on the critical list and for several months after that remained as a convalescent. By the next spring he was allowed some limited exercise which helped get him well enough, as far as the prison authorities were concerned, for him to be sent straight back into the foul atmosphere of the tinsmithing foundry again. The almost immediate deterioration in his condition then forced his move outside and he was set to stone-dressing.

Throughout all this, as the seasons and the years dragged away, he had kept up his efforts at petitioning for release or, at the least, a review of his case and sentence. Now, suddenly, he found he wasn't alone in his efforts. He found that his brother had been campaigning non-stop in Australia for his release and Witton, from whom mail had been withheld for a considerable time, got from that brother a letter and a copy of an opinion given by one of Australia's leading legal minds, Isaac Isaacs, destined to become Chief Justice and later Governor-General.

The opinion was clear that there were grounds for the King to review the whole case and to pardon Witton, and there were petitions being raised in Australia and in South Africa supporting that. Leading politicians and public figures in both countries, churchmen, citizens of all kinds, even some of the Boer generals, signed the petitions. But to no effect until in 1904 a member of the Cape Town legislature, J. D. Logan, who had a home in Scotland, visited England and began personally lobbying in Westminster. It seemed to be the final small push needed, a single voice topping the 100 000 signatures from Australia and the many from South Africa. Within days Logan was given custody of Witton and a few weeks later, while Witton was enjoying Logan's hospitality in Scotland, the formal discharge arrived.

So the death sentence had been commuted to life imprisonment, which had come down to something close to three years during which time the Boer War had ended, the King had been crowned, Witton's father had died without his son knowing of it, and illness and imprisonment had reduced a sturdy young soldier to a thin and pallid man in an illcut suit and a pair of clumsy boots, a bowler hat set awkwardly on a head on which the hair was still very short.

Back in Australia Witton settled in Gippsland, on the fertile southern plains of Victoria, going back to the farming from which he had originally broken away. In the late 1920s he wrote his book *Scapegoats of the Empire*, a highly-personalised account of the events before, during, and after the courts martial and of his life in prison. It is undoubtedly biased, but it was for many years the nearest thing we had to a true account of what happened and it has long formed the basis for many of the ideas which have sprung around those events and for much of what appeared in my novel.

In his letter to Thomas in 1929 Witton harks back again to the shooting of the missionary, Heese. He says 'But you must not forget Kitchener held Handcock's "confession" in which he implicated me as an accessory no doubt unwittingly done while in a high shivery (?) nervous state—but that accounts for the reason why only Morant, Handcock and myself were punished and the War Office so adamant in my case. Had there been no Hesse case the shooting of prisoners would not have worried them much. But the shooting of Hesse was a premeditated and most cold-blooded affair. Handcock with his own lips described it all to me. I consider I am the one and only one that suffered unjustly (apart from yourself). Morant and Handcock being acquitted my lips were sealed.'

And, apart from getting it all off his chest in his book, his lips stayed sealed. He left the dairy farm before the first World War — in which he took no part — and moved north to Brisbane where he married and lived quietly. There were no children and when his wife died Witton moved south again to Drouin, in Victoria, where he managed a butter factory and lived with his nephew until he died on 15 August 1942. Thomas outlived him by only a few weeks but, of the Bush Veldt Carbineer officers who stood trial in 1902 (unless Picton survived him), George Ramsdale Witton clung longest to life.

ROBERT LENEHAN

There are two sections of the Army Act in force in 1902 worth looking at.

Section 26: Every person subject to Military Law who commits any of the following offences, that is to say: —
(2) Refuses or by culpable neglect omits to make or send a report or return which it is his duty to make or send, shall on conviction by Court Martial be liable, if an Officer, to be cashiered, *or to suffer such less punishment as in this Act mentioned.* [My italics].

Section 44: Punishment may be inflicted in respect of offences committed by persons subject to military law and convicted by Courts Martial: —

In the case of Officers, according to the scale following:
a. Death
b. Penal servitude for a term not less than 3 years.
c. Imprisonment, with or without hard labour, for a term not exceeding two years.
d. Cashiering.
e. Dismissal from Her Majesty's service.
f. Forfeiture in the prescribed manner of seniority of rank, either in the Army or in the Corps to which the offender belongs, or in both.
g. Reprimand, or severe reprimand.

There were two Charge Sheets against Lenehan, each of them citing his 'culpable neglect' in the terms of A.A. 26. He was cleared on one of those charges and found guilty on the other. The sentence was 'To be reprimanded'. That was the least severe punishment he could have been awarded; beyond that there could only be a dismissal of the charges. In that light it seems remarkable that the Provost Marshal in Pretoria should have received a 'Pressing & Confidential' signal saying, in its final paragraph, 'The finding and sentence of the Court in the case of Major Lenehan will be promulgated as soon as practicable after his arrival and he is then to be despatched to Cape Town and embarked for Australia as quickly as possible. Will you be so good as to *take steps to have him carefully supervised until he actually sails.*' [My italics].

It is certain that Lenehan was an angry man. His military efficiency and honour had been impugned, his unit disbanded, his officers tried and savagely sentenced. He had been subjected to weeks of close confinement and was now under guard and to be shipped home from the war with no greater stain against him than the minor one of a reprimand. He was determined not to let the matter rest there and when he got home to Australia he began a battle royal. Lenehan was in one corner; in the other was Edward Hutton, Major-General.

They make an interesting study in contrasts. Lenehan, first gazetted as a Provisional Lieutenant in October 1890; Hutton, who by then had served as an officer in the Zulu War in the previous year and who went on to see action in the first clash with the Boers in 1881 and 1882, against the Ahmed-Arabi in Egypt later in 1882, and in the Nile Expedition and the campaign in the Sudan a couple of years later.

Lenehan's record of service shows his promotions to Lieutenant in the 1st. Infantry Regiment in New South Wales in 1892, to Captain four years later in the N.S.W. Field Artillery, and to Major in that same regiment in 1898. His listing appears after the letter 'M' for Militia (Hutton was the fully-professional soldier).

Lenehan was a burly and commanding figure, full of presence, whereas Hutton was described by a contemporary as 'a fiery little English soldier of whom even his most outspoken critics readily admitted his ability'. There was little doubt of that. He was sent out to Australia as a Temporary Major-General in 1893, at the age of 55, to command the military forces of New South Wales, then still a Colony, and he strongly fostered the idea of mounted infantry. He did an excellent job and commanded many of those Australians in the Boer War when, as a Brigadier again, he led a mixed force of about 6000 Mounted Infantry from Britain, Canada, Australia, and New Zealand. The four men who were to stand trial and receive punishment were in that command—and so was Lenehan. Somewhere along the way, either during 'Curly' Hutton's period in New South Wales or in the field in South Africa, Lenehan crossed his path, did something to excite the dislike of this 'fiery little English soldier', and the effects were far-reaching.

In 1902 the new Commonwealth Government of Australia invited Hutton back to shape the diverse military establishments of the previous Colonies into a unified system. By that time Lenehan had begun his campaign—questions had been asked in the Parliament and the press had picked up the matter. Lenehan reported to Hutton and, I suspect to his surprise, was met with little sympathy. Whatever had passed between the two men before, Hutton now obviously felt scandalised that such things should have happened in a British military force and felt, too, that the whole affair could only bring Australia's soldiers into disrepute. He advised Lenehan to keep quiet about it all until some information could be got from South Africa.

It has to be remembered that, until Lenehan's return to his home country, virtually nothing was known there about the courts martial and the consequences; Handcock's widow was still in ignorance of her husband's death. However, Hutton could not simply refuse Lenehan's right to approach the Prime Minister, Sir Edmund Barton, but he stipulated that it should be a private and unofficial approach. Parliamentary questions and the intervention of Barton led to a response from Kitchener, a long telegram which presented a strangely inaccurate version of what had happened.

Kitchener cabled that there had been twenty separate murders on specific dates and with no extenuating circumstances; there was not that number of murder charges, neither was Morant within many kilometres of the Spelonken on one of the dates mentioned. Kitchener claimed there was no ill-treatment of Hunt's body, a fact which had been disproven in the court; and it is hardly likely that so many recommendations to mercy would have been made by the court had there been no extenuating circumstances.

In the build-up of interest and publicity Hutton advised Lenehan to resign. Lenehan refused and asked for a Court of Inquiry to which Hutton responded by telling him that if he would not resign within a day he would be dismissed from the service. And there began an exchange of correspondence which is remarkable for the virulence of tone on Hutton's part and his almost savage insistence on getting Lenehan out of military service.

To the Secretary of Defence, 13 May 1902: 'I have the honour to recommend that Major R. W. Lenehan . . . should be retired from the Military Services of the Commonwealth. Major Lenehan who has been reprimanded for culpable neglect in connection with such serious and peculiarly disgraceful events in the Regiment under his command, and who has since had his services dispensed with in

South Africa, is in my opinion unfitted to retain his position on the Active List . . . An opportunity has been given to Major Lenehan to resign his commission in the New South Wales Artillery which he has declined to avail himself of, and I now recommend that he be retired. An Order in Council is attached.'

It must have been disappointing to Hutton that nothing happened. In August a paragraph appeared in a Sydney newspaper which said, 'Major R. W. Lenehan, who is to recount his South African campaign experiences in the Centenary Hall on Tuesday night, has had a long experience as a soldier . . . (he) should certainly have an interesting story to tell.'

Whatever the story was it excited Hutton into another letter to the Secretary of Defence, dated 7 August. He first referred to his earlier minute, then went on: 'I regret to say that this Officer has committed the indiscretion of delivering a lecture . . . in Sydney, which considering the position that he holds in regard to his services having been dispensed with by the Commander-in-Chief in South Africa, can only be characterised in all respects as reprehensible. I would again urgently request that the Order in Council submitted on 13th. May for the retirement of this Officer should receive the early and favourable consideration of the Minister. The retention of this Officer . . . reflects in a most serious degree upon the honour of the Military Forces of the Commonwealth under my command.'

In the middle of all this there was a memorandum from the Military Pay Office in Sydney to the Military Secretary in which the question of whether Lenehan should be paid as an Officer of the 2nd. Contingent Mounted Infantry or not is raised. There is the charming phrase, 'It is rumoured that . . . (he) . . . left his Regiment early in the present year and took charge of the Bushveldt Carbineers . . .'

The Acting Staff Paymaster, the Assistant Adjutant-General, the Military Secretary, and the Acting Commandant to The Principal Under-Secretary all got involved and a coded cablegram was eventually sent to Cape Town, a cable which began with the disarming address, 'Cheatingly, Capetown' and went on 'Has Major Lenehan left levelism handful and joined Bushveldt Carbineers gissiplike covertly bigotries luxurious our imposingly'. I don't have the decoded version but I like to think the reply also made use of such words as 'covertly', 'bigotries', and 'imposingly'. They seem singularly appropriate!

Meantime Hutton hadn't given up. He wrote again to the Secretary of Defence on 19 November repeating all his earlier statements and saying that Lenehan had been given 'the option of voluntarily resigning . . . under the discreditable circumstances referred to'. Again, it needs to be clearly remembered that Lenehan had only been reprimanded.

Five days after that Lenehan wrote to the Staff Office of the Defence Forces, Australia: 'Sir, The Daily Telegraph newspaper of Sydney published on the 9th. instant a statement purporting to come from the Honourable the Minister for Defence Commonwealth Forces that he then had under consideration my case as to whether I should cease to belong to the Commonwealth Forces. It is my desire to be heard in my own defence on the subject of any charge against me before my case be dealt with. As this matter is according to the Newspaper statement now before the Minister for Defence I ask that this letter be forwarded to him through the G.O.C. Commonwealth Forces.'

The letter *was* forwarded, eventually reached the Minister, and drew from him a request from Hutton for information. That resulted in yet another of the General's minutes in which he made much of the fact that Lenehan had been under escort, in close arrest, and confined as an 'ordinary prisoner' in Cape Town, and suggested that Kitchener be approached to see whether *he* thought the Major a fit person to retain in the service.

By mid-December of 1902 it seemed that Hutton was backing into a corner, forced by adherence to correct procedure to take an action he did not approve. But he managed to recover some ground. He forwarded Lenehan's application to be heard in his own defence, but then added, 'I see no object in calling on this Officer for any statement of the kind inasmuch as there is no charge against him that I am aware of. His services have been dispensed with by the C-in-C in South Africa and on that account I have recommended that he should be placed on the retired list . . .'

The battle went on. In March 1903 Hutton wrote directly to the new Minister of Defence, Sir John Forrest.

'My Dear Sir John,
I have no hesitation whatever in emphasizing the views I have already sent you officially regarding this Officer and his conduct in South Africa. I enclose you typewritten copies of the two latest so as to save your looking up the files of correspondence upon this unhappy case.

'Major Lenehan was to have been tried for his life, as his attitude towards Lieut. Morant and those concerned in the murders of the prisoners in cold blood was such as to justify the belief that he was a particeps criminis. Sufficient evidence upon this was not however forthcoming and he was tried upon the lesser charge.

'Apart from Major Lenehan's conduct as Commanding Officer of this unhappy Corps of Bushveldt Carbineers I have the very poorest opinion of this Officer's qualifications as an officer. He served under my command while I was in N.S.W. 93–96, and also upon active service in South Africa when he commanded a squadron of the N.S.W. Mounted Rifles. I have never heard a good word said for him either in Peace or War.'

It seems to be a peculiarly savage attack from a senior officer upon a junior one, and it clearly cut little ice with the practical and level-headed Forrest. He sent a minute to his Secretary, saying, 'As far as can be ascertained, all there is against Major Lenehan is that he was tried by Court Martial for neglect of duty and was "reprimanded" which appears to be the lightest penalty awarded. It seems rather unjust to punish this officer again by retiring him and I am inclined not to take any steps in that direction. Before submitting the matter to Cabinet with a recommendation, please refer again to the General Officer Commanding.'

Hutton would not be deterred. He went on writing to the Secretary of Defence, another reiteration of his argument in May 1903, while Forrest sent in a long and very detailed report to the Prime Minister and Cabinet . . . It covered all the ground previously ploughed so exhaustively by Hutton but in a clear and dispassionate fashion, and commented on the meagre information supplied by the War Office—and it seemed to come down on Hutton's side at the end. The final paragraph reads, 'The weak spot in this case is that Major Lenehan has never made any communication to the Government complaining of the treatment he received in South Africa, but appears to have accepted the finding of the Court, and taken his stand on the fact that he has already been punished by being "reprimanded" for the offence with which he was charged, and that he should not be punished again. It cannot, however, be overlooked that he was removed under arrest from South Africa, and virtually returned to Australia in disgrace; and unless he is able to show that the treatment he received was unjust, it is difficult to see how he can expect to be re-instated in command of Australian troops. If he is content to sit still under what he may consider injustice, and make no personal effort to clear himself, he must put up with the consequences.'

But whatever happened to the old concept of 'double jeopardy', and to Lenehan's requests for a Court of Inquiry to clear himself? Well, the Prime Minister wrote to the Governor-General, Baron Tennyson, including a request that he cable London for copies of the

COMMONWEALTH DEFENCE.

No. .... 190 .

Minute Paper for the Executive Council.

RECOMMENDED FOR THE APPROVAL OF HIS EXCELLENCY THE GOVERNOR-GENERAL IN COUNCIL.

C O M M O N W E A L T H   M I L I T A R Y   F O R C E S.

N E W   S O U T H   W A L E S.

APPOINTMENT OF OFFICERS SERVING ON THE 30th JUNE, 1903, IN UNITS UNDER THE OLD ORGANIZATION, TO UNITS UNDER NOMENCLATURE OF THE NEW ORGANIZATION.

That the appointment of the undermentioned Officer serving on the 30th June, 1903, in Unit under the Old Organization to Unit under nomenclature of the New Organization, as published in the Commonwealth of Australia Gazette of the 25th July, 1903, be approved.

Appointment to bear date 1st July, 1903.

Reserve of Officers ~~UNATTACHED LIST~~.

Major Robert William Lenehan from the New South Wales Artillery (Field).

Retype please as amended

3/8/02

Minister of State for Defence.

Approved by His Excellency the Governor-General in Council, and entered on the Minutes of the Executive Council accordingly.

Clerk of the Council.

Gazetted..........

846

A photostat copy of the Minute changing Lenehan from the Unattached List to the Reserve of Officers

Court Martial evidence against Lenehan. The Under-Secretary of State for the Colonies replied, sending a copy of those proceedings — and all that seems to have happened is the preparation of two Minute Papers for the Executive Council, each of them dealing with the general subject of the appointment of officers serving in units under the old system to the units established within the new organisation — Hutton's organisation.

One Minute lists the appointment from 1 July 1903 of Major Robert William Lenehan to the Australian Field Artillery (New South Wales); the other lists Major Robert William Lenehan from the New South Wales Artillery (Field) to the 'Unattached List'. Those last words are inked over and written in their place are the words 'Reserve of Officers'. Neither minute is signed.

In October 1903 Hutton took a sideswipe at James Francis Thomas. In yet another note to the Secretary for Defence he wrote: 'I have the honour to state for the information of the Minister that if it is the intention of Captain and Honorary Major Thomas, Reserve of Officers, New South Wales, to publish matter impugning the decision of the Court Martial held upon G. R. Whitton [*sic*] . . . it would be well for this Officer to forward his resignation in anticipation of such statements.' This was a skirmish which Hutton won, for Thomas did, indeed, resign his commission.

By April of 1904 the tide was turning against Hutton. The Minister for Defence then was Austin Chapman and he wrote, quite coldly, '. . . it would seem that he (Lenehan) has suffered additional punishment . . . beyond the sentence of the Court-Martial. On the other hand, if this treatment was on account of rumours as to which possibly there was no evidence, then it is equally contrary to principles of justice. Whichever view is taken, I cannot see my way to sanction the removal of Major Lenehan from the Forces on account of anything that appeared in the evidence before the Court-Martial. Being thus thrown back upon that evidence, I find that his judges considered a reprimand sufficient punishment for the offence there disclosed. It would be manifestly unjust were I, upon the same evidence, to recommend his removal from his own Forces in respect to what was considered adequate punishment by a mere reprimand by a tribunal of the Forces in which he was then serving.'

A month later there was a new Minister, Senator Dawson, and he wrote simply: '. . . I consider that Major Lenehan should now be restored to his position in the New South Wales Forces and an Order in Council be submitted to give effect to this.' The Secretary wrote to Hutton saying that 'the Minister wishes his instructions to be at once carried out . . .'

A photostat copy of the telegram sent by the G.O.C., Maj.-Gen. Hutton, to Gen. Finn inferring ulterior motives to Lenehan's request for leave

It may have seemed to be the end of it, but Hutton, like a bulldog with his jaw locked into his victim's throat, appeared incapable of letting go. He sent a request through channels to General Finn at Army HQ in Sydney asking him to ascertain 'present position and status if honourable of Lenehan'. Those words 'if honourable' have a strong emotional loading, but Hutton's delaying tactic caused the Minister to go no further pending the result of the enquiries.

At that time family affairs took Lenehan away from Sydney and high up on the north coast, and Finn wired Hutton that there was a request from Lenehan for six months' leave. Hutton wrote back in terms which I consider to be disgraceful and unworthy of the man: 'Direct General Finn to report confidentially and if necessary investigate circumstances which necessitate Officer have six months leave. I have reason to believe Officer has acted dishonestly in regard to money entrusted to him and Colonel Onslow can throw light on circumstances. Inform Minister that I have directed further investigation and that Officer's integrity and present circumstances require full report and investigation as above before any further action by Government. State also I fully adhere to opinion expressed regarding this Officer.'

A story had gained some small circulation—a rumour about Lenehan's legal office and a trust fund. Three officers, Colonels Onslow and Waddell and Major Freehill, had apparently indulged in some gossip about this. Word had leaked back to Hutton, thus that message which drew some unwelcome responses. The Deputy Adjutant-General telegraphed, 'General Finn reports verbally that Onslow's statement is merely hearsay and refers to matter at least five years old. Major Freehill states honesty unquestioned.' From Senator Dawson came the curt request, 'Re Lenehan wish to be informed on what grounds you made statement re integrity Lenehan.' And from the Acting Secretary, Department of Defence, 'With reference to your telegram of the 3rd. inst., relative to Major Lenehan, I am directed to inform you that the Minister has made the following minute thereon:—

"I desire to express my entire disapproval of the manner in which the General Officer Commanding, by means of a confidential communication reflected on the integrity of Major Lenehan on what appears to have been unreliable information, and for the acceptance of which the General Officer Commanding is responsible. Unnecessary delay occurred in carrying out my instructions of the 23rd. May; and so far I do not consider that the General Officer Commanding has afforded any satisfactory explanation".' That reprimand—for it was all of that—landed on Hutton's desk in mid-August.

In the following month the Minister—another new one—sent a confidential memo to Hutton, marked 'Urgent'. It was a précis of Lenehan's original conversation with the General on his return to Australia, and it also raised the matter of a claim of £1100 against the Imperial Government. Hutton was asked to give the matter his prompt attention and he fired his final salvo: 'Major Lenehan states the facts in a manner calculated to mislead . . . I have taken no action against Major Lenehan in regard to his conduct in South Africa . . . (he) is not a fit and proper person to hold a commission . . .' Hutton attached *all* his previous correspondence and asked for it to be sent to the Secretary of State for War and for him to judge.

It did not work. Two-and-a-half years of persistent and deliberate attempts to get Lenehan out of the Army and an overt attempt to prove him dishonest—none of it worked. It is possible to assume that Hutton was moved only by high principles, that he was concerned only with protecting what he saw as the honour of the Australian forces. It is possible that he honestly felt that Lenehan's actions in South Africa really made him unfit to command, despite

Lenehan (in pith helmet) while training troops for action in Mesopotamia during the first World War *(Photo: Courtesy of Lenehan family)*

the light sentence imposed on him. It is also possible that the General (and perhaps Kitchener above him) had a personal antipathy towards the Major, for certainly the tone of his correspondence indicates something more than an official and military viewpoint. But none of it worked.

Hutton went back to England in time for Christmas of 1904. He took command of the 3rd Division there and was in administrative charge of Eastern Command; he retired as Lieutenant-General in 1907. At the outbreak of the Great War he volunteered for service again and was charged with raising and organising the 21st Division of Third Army. He died in Torquay in August 1923.

But the apparent vendetta against Lenehan bore some fruit. Although he had retained his rank as Major in the Australian Field Artillery, Lenehan's attempts to go overseas with an active command in the Great War were refused, and he and his family and friends always felt it was in part a legacy of Hutton's work and in part a refusal by Kitchener to accept him for active service. However true or untrue that may be, in 1913 he was promoted to Lieutenant-Colonel in the 4th Australian Field Artillery Brigade and was Acting Brigadier, with the task of training and preparing other men to go overseas. His depot was on the outer edge of Sydney and a good part of his work was involved with troops destined for Mesopotamia.

Imaginatively, he moved a number of camels into the camp to accustom both soldiers and horses to them, and he had the reputation of being both an efficient and a popular officer.

He was an imposing figure, a little Blimpish in shape and appearance, a strict disciplinarian when necessary, and still with an excellent seat on a horse. In his non-military life his legal practice followed a quietly prosperous course and he became involved with some other Sydney businessmen and philanthropists in the formation of The Millions Club, an informal organisation self-charged with promoting migration to Australia from Britain—and so increasing the millions in its population.

He was ill several times with a chest complaint and in 1922, when he was about to leave for his son's property at Emerald Hill in the north of the State, he collapsed with a severe attack of pneumonia from which he never recovered. He died a year before Hutton.

JAMES FRANCIS THOMAS

No matter the outcome of the courts martial there is no way in which James Francis Thomas could have been accused of failure as an advocate. When he took on the defence brief his charges had already been subjected to twelve weeks of close, generally solitary, confinement. They were considerably bewildered by having been passed from Court of Inquiry to Court Martial and they had almost no time for consultation with this stranger-lawyer.

Equally, he had no clear knowledge at the outset of the ramifications of the charges, either in the military or the legal sense, and no personal knowledge of the men concerned—with the possible exception of Lenehan. Neither had he had courtroom experience. Yet, in spite of all that, he put up an amazingly good effort when the gravity of the charges and the nature of the evidence is considered. He pleaded cogently and successfully enough to get Lenehan no more than a reprimand; to get the others acquitted entirely on one charge; and, when the Court came to sentencing, three of the accused were recommended to mercy—a recommendation that was surely based on Thomas's pleas. But there was no way he could clear them all, no way he could save Morant and Handcock from that morning parade when they stared down the muzzles of a row of rifles.

He was a changed man when he got home to Australia. Like so many young men of the pre-war Volunteers he had found the massive difference between soldiering at home in peace-time and overseas in war to be the difference between a social parade and a surprise attack that left blood on the hands and dead on the ground.

That, plus the events of the courts martial and their grim aftermath, had brought a sombre tone into his life with an undertone which seemed at times to amount to a quiet frenzy.

He was obviously an intelligent man and well versed in his profession so it is not very likely that he saw grave injustices in the actual administering of the military code of law at the trials, although it is sure enough that he felt there were inconsistencies; but mature consideration must have shown him that what was done in the courtroom was, overall, properly enough done. His own performance had included some lapses; remember the comment from the Judge-Advocate-General's review that, '. . . a heap of irrelevant evidence was admitted by the Court on the part of the defence despite

J. F. Thomas, stiff in a brand-new uniform, on the day he was promoted to First Lieutenant (*Photo: Author's collection*)

the ruling of the Judge Advocate . . .' To Thomas, though, the two salient facts were that the prisoners had been accused of doing what many others had done without being brought to trial and that the executions of Morant and Handcock were far too severe as punishment.

The Bathurst *National Advocate* of 2 April 1902 published a letter from Thomas in which he said: 'It was proved that in other cases exactly the same procedure was adopted and approved of by other officers. Consequently you will see that from a soldier's point of view, at any rate, the crime was not so dreadful as might appear, although technically it was a crime.

'I only regret that poor Morant and Handcock did not receive a sentence of penal servitude, but, poor fellows, they were shot at about eighteen hours notice. Over Handcock's death I have suffered the deepest grief. It may be that before long I shall be back in Australia, when I shall make it my business to let the Government know the position. As counsel . . . I should like to see that all the facts from the prisoners' point of view are fairly brought forward. When everything is known you will not think the disgrace amounts to much or anything. War is war, and rough things have to be done. Only yesterday news came in of horrible barbarities on the part of the Boers towards some of our colonials. I say, they deserve all they (the Boers) get, and with less nonsense and sentiment the war would be over.'

It was an attitude from which he never departed. An old Tenterfield resident wrote, 'It has been suggested that the Handcock and Morant incident affected his mind. I would not go so far as to say that, but the old hands have often said that Thomas was never the same man. Mention of the South African War is sufficient to give him a glint in his eye and if one is prepared to listen to his usually long and discursive monologue one cannot help being interested in what he has to say.'

With Lenehan and Witton back in Australia, Thomas was peripherally involved with their attempts to clear their own names and he opened a correspondence with Witton. One letter may help to solve the problem of what happened to the papers and records of the courts martial which Thomas said he had brought back with him. Witton wrote to him: 'I would very much like to peruse the evidence of the Hesse trial although I took no part in it or was present. If you have a copy and would care to send it to me I would take particular care of it and return it safely.' There has to be a reasonable chance that Thomas *did* send all the papers to Witton and that they were never returned or were lost somehow in the post. Witton's quite detailed account of the proceedings in the court must have been based on something more than his memory, and Thomas's papers would have been ideal material for him.

But there were other things to be attended to—there was his legal practice and his newspaper, the leader columns of which he was still using for political purposes. He was a staunch advocate of the move for a separate State of New England and he was also one of the prime movers behind a new party with leanings toward socialist policies and decentralisation. One of his editorials said: '. . . there is the ever increasing trend of the rural population towards the cities . . . the voice of the small bush newspaper is very much that of one crying in the wilderness, but nevertheless its cry at all times should be directed against the blighting evil of city congestion.'

He saw the formation of the new party, the Country Party, and, too, saw it develop into a strong but hardly socialist group, with such an effective hold on rural voting blocs that it was able eventually to become part of the conservative coalition government and to have a very muscular grip on national policies.

By the outbreak of the first World War Thomas was fifty-three, a solidly-built man deeply settled into the life of his town and district, and a considerable mover and shaper of local events. He was also well settled into a fairly bad financial position. The newspaper's demands on his time meant a deal of neglect of his legal work; neither task could be done properly and both suffered as a result, as did his income. Add to that his generosity toward all sorts of causes and it can be seen that his decision to sell the *Star* in 1915 was largely forced upon him. He went back to the law but still not to that alone, for he had a small property at Boonoo Boonoo, a little out of Tenterfield, where he farmed in a minor way and grew a fine garden; and he maintained a very strong interest in the local military unit as well as doing much research and writing for the Historical Society.

John Dearden, a historian of the area, has written, 'After Federation and the reorganisation of the Australian Defence Forces the Tenterfield Half Squadron became No. 1 Half Squadron of the 6th Australian Light Horse. The members formed a club known as the Mounted Rifle Club . . . and of this club J. F. Thomas was appointed Trustee and also Patron. It was as Trustee that he was able to assist with the fund-raising and building of the Memorial Front to the Drill Hall which exists to this day, and as Patron assisted in fund-raising to finance the 1910 and 1912 Prince of Wales Cup teams. He did maintain his interest in the Unit until the last. I well remember him coming quietly into the Club meetings and sitting back, keeping in touch with the progress of the troop, but taking no active part. He

Three troopers of the Tenterfield Light Horse at the railway station on their way to the war (*Photo: Author's collection*)

was held in high esteem by members of the Light Horse troop, firstly as a soldier and an Officer during the earlier days of the Unit, and for his assistance in establishing a museum at the Memorial Hall.'

High esteem, but low finances. And, it seems, with a strong aversion towards government interference into his private affairs;

and that included, apparently, assessments for taxation. Indeed, his whole attitude towards money seems to have been a bit cavalier. There are some interesting sidelights on that in a long letter about the man written in 1939 by a fellow-solicitor in Tenterfield, Edgar Jennings. Here are some extracts.

'There is no doubt as to the townmanship and public spiritedness of his early days. He was a moving spirit in most public affairs in Tenterfield and very liberal in supporting them both with money and energy. The energy was his own but there are grave doubts whether that applied to the money. The old hands have often told me how they would go into his office and find him surrounded with heaps of documents and papers in every conceivable part of the room which would support a document or paper. One had only to mention a matter possibly years old when Thomas had the uncanny faculty of being able to put his hands straight-way onto the file.

'He would also work night after night until well after midnight and would be seen leaving his office to walk to his farm some three or four miles from Tenterfield. He used to take a short cut through the local cemetery and when exhaustion overtook him would rest his head on a tombstone, snatch a sleep and afterwards continue his journey to arrive at his farm about daylight when, more often than not, he would hack a piece of bread from a loaf, seize an onion or anything else which may have been handy for his breakfast and set about the return walk to his office.

'Old clients often walked in to find him asleep in the office chair with his head resting on a bundle of papers or perhaps stretched out on an old couch with a saddle for a pillow. As a lawyer he was no doubt one of ability and astute, but I waver between the opinion that he was either rankly dishonest or a dangerous muddler when I come to consider some of the things he has done while carrying on his profession.'

It is the picture of an ageing and eccentric man, a man who by the time Edgar Jennings wrote those words had already been struck off the Rolls and disbarred from legal practice. After repeated refusals to allow public examination of his property and assets for taxation purposes, and for the payment of a debt, Thomas then disobeyed a Court Order, was taken to trial, and sentenced to a term of imprisonment in Long Bay Gaol.

Mr W. P. Walters, now retired to Goonellabah in New South Wales, remembers that time in this fashion: 'I was a law clerk in the employ of a well-known Sydney firm in 1928. My firm acted as Sydney Agents for a great number of country solicitors and Thomas was one of them, although very little work came to us from him.

'I presume that some time after he was committed to prison Thomas sent a message to my firm to the effect that he needed some assistance. As I was in charge of all the firm's Sydney Agency work, I was sent to see him at Long Bay. I recall that I made a number of visits by tram to the jail and that he occupied a fairly large room there set up as an office, that he had there the usual office files of a solicitor, that he gave me many draft letters and documents for typing and that he shunned my suggestion that he get himself released from prison by filing a voluntary bankruptcy petition. In fact I think it was he who told me this could be done. I really don't know whether Thomas was a man of high principles or just plain stubborn.

'I have a clear recollection of one of my visits when a prison warder knocked at the open doorway and said, "Morning tea is ready Mr. Thomas". Thomas excused himself and trotted off. That did not strike me as being true prison life at all.'

He spent a year in Long Bay and then the N.S.W. Attorney-General had him declared bankrupt and he was released. It may have been courage or obstinacy — and he had plenty of both — but he went back to Tenterfield to live, an ex-prisoner about whom stories of malpractice were already circulating, unable to practise law, financially insecure. He still had his property at Boonoo Boonoo, he still, undoubtedly, had the affection of the members of the Club and of old soldiers of Boer War days, but he was hardly the man he had been, physically or socially.

Here is Edgar Jennings again: 'How he exists is a little puzzling. I understand that he collects the rents from a few old Estates in the case of absent Trustees or beneficiaries and also has an Insurance Agency. I do not think the commissions from these collections would maintain him. In fact one absent beneficiary had great difficulty in obtaining from Thomas an accounting of the rents he had collected. That fact may be a possible explanation of how he lives.

'His mode of living is certainly eccentric. I do not think he eats with the regularity of the average individual, but when hungry he possibly pulls a carrot out of a small vegetable garden he has and chews that. He is a bachelor, a member of the Historical Society and he has a complex to champion the cause of the underdog.

'Although at one time it could be said that he was the leading citizen of the town with the respect and esteem of all classes, nowadays he makes very little contact with his fellow men. I am inclined to believe that the attitude of mind towards him of the majority is one of pity in seeing a man of his unquestionable attainments drift lower and lower in the scale of civilization.

'I might say that the legal affairs of this town will be in some instances chaotic when Thomas dies because many details are stored at the back of his mind and that is the only record of them. His memory is exceptional. One has only to ask him the details of some transaction that happened years ago and if Thomas wants to he will be able to relate the details with a great degree of accuracy.

'You will note that I have said if Thomas *wants* to. I do this because there are many details of past events which if forgotten would add greatly to his comfort.'

When that was written Thomas, 'old J. F.' as he was by then generally known, was seventy-eight, stooped and gaunt, and with a rather odd gait. Some years earlier he had been operated on for a kidney ailment and had to suffer the awkward indignity of wearing a rubber bag inside his trousers with a tube into his stomach; he walked oddly in an attempt to pretend the unsightly bulge was not there. He was by then very much a loner, quiet and unspeaking when he sat at the back of Club meetings, exchanging the barest courtesies when he crabbed along Tenterfield's streets, living with a frugality which would have alarmed an ascetic monk. But he was always neat, even in clothes which became increasingly shabby. His shoes were always clean and his appearance as close to dapper as his grossly reduced circumstances would allow. He kept his reticence and privacy until the very end, on Armistice Day 1942, during the third war in his lifetime.

In Column 5 of the Death Certificate, under the heading 'Cause of Death', there is entered, 'la-Uraemia; lb-Chronic Nephritis; lc-Hypertrophied Prostate; 2-Malnutrition.' That certificate tells of a sad end to a life of action and passion. There is a cruelty about a man of obvious intellect and strength of conviction finishing his time so broken — in body by neglect and hunger; in mind undoubtedly affected by the stresses set up during a few miserable weeks in South Africa forty years earlier.

Of all the men involved in these trials only two, Morant and Handcock, were quickly dead. It is possible that some few of them were yet to die in the last of the fighting in South Africa; many of them would go on — members of the Court, witnesses, observers, attendants, gaolers — to suffer or to die in the Great War. Some of them would live for long years and into the second World War, seeing in the arc of time how the savage actions of the century's start were more savagely surpassed.

But the rattle of rifle-fire which killed Morant and Handcock left long-lasting and often strange echoes.

More than seven years later, after a welter of official correspondence and a seemingly-endless series of questions, compensation was paid to relatives of some of the Boers who had been killed by the BVC. The Army Council agreed to funds being made available through the Treasury and payments ranging upwards from £100 were paid. One or two went to twice that amount and one widow, Mrs Geyser, received £1000, although her claim was for considerably more.

When the six Boers were killed it was said that there was something like £800 in rough gold in their wagon. No trace of it was ever found but there was a strong suspicion (never confirmed) that the enigmatic Captain Taylor had got away with it. The body of the Reverend Mr Heese was removed and given new burial after a memorial attendance. It lies now where it was re-interred at his old Mission Station at Makapaanspoort in Northern Transvaal.

The Bush Veldt Carbineers ceased to exist. The unit lived for a

```
        Claim for Compensation by Mrs M. M. Geyser as
   Surviving Spouse of the late J. J. Geyser Sr.


To  2 Waggons with —— trek Gear complete    £120. 0. 0
    75 Head of Cattle mixed                  750. 0. 0
    2 Salted Riding Horses                    40. 0. 0
    2 Salted Mules                            50. 0. 0
    8 Bags Wheat                              20. 0. 0
       Clothing, Bedding and Sundries         25. 0. 0
       Cash which the deceased took with
       him when he left Pietersburg
            Gold      £35.0.0
        about G.Notes 190.0.0
            Rough Gold 150.0.0               375. 0. 0
                                          £1,450. 0. 0

             (Sgd) M. M. GEYSER.
```

A photostat copy of one of the many claims for compensation lodged by families of Boers disadvantaged by the fighting

short while under the new identity of the Pietersburg Light Horse and appears for the first and last time under that name in the Army List of April 1902. Whether as BVC or PLH it was a strange and doomed corps of soldiers with never a badge or crest of its own, no colours, no uniform, and no tradition. It was born of expediency, lived a dark life, and died in disgrace.

Kitchener came out of it all well. His political masters approved and supported his actions and, after the first startled responses from the press, there was a general tone of agreement with what he had ordered. The London *Daily Mail* declared: 'The guilt of the BVC, an irregular corps of horsemen, casts no stain upon the conduct of the war or upon the British Army'... which may be one way of saying that no one in South Africa but the BVC was responsible for desperate deeds. The appropriate Biblical quotation would seem to be the unctuous 'God, I thank thee that I am not as other men are...'

The *Daily News* said: 'Even the minimum of the facts of the case shows that Lord Kitchener is a just and fearless commander.' In the *Standard* it was said that '... misleading statements with regard to the execution of the officers have fostered a misunderstanding with Australia but the facts of the case will ultimately show that the guilty men were treated with the utmost equity.' The *St James Gazette* managed a double by saying that '... the justice meted out by Lord Kitchener has vindicated the honor of the British Army, and declares that Australia should not be held responsible for the misdeeds of the irregular troops.' Even hostile foreign voices were satisfactorily quietened as, for example, the *Mail and Express* of New York which helped satisfy diplomatic needs by saying, 'The course taken by Lord Kitchener will prevent the incident being charged against England.' The *Pall Mall Gazette* weighed in with a rather smug piece of editorialising which said, in part, '... the exemplary punishment of the guilty men will convince the Boers that even-handed justice is a characteristic of the British nation.'

The Times took it upon itself to speak for Australia: 'It is wholly incorrect and misleading to speak of the guilty men as Australian officers, as the squadron to which they were attached did not form part of the splendid Australian contingent which has won so much distinction during the course of the campaign. We are confident that the Australians as a whole will endorse the general judgment of the Empire in regard to this deplorable affair when the facts are disclosed.' It was a pious hope which proved untrue, largely because the facts were disclosed only piecemeal and reluctantly.

Witton, Lenehan, and Thomas kept the affair alive and frequently kicking hard, and the more that was heard in Australia the less well-regarded the British actions became. Kitchener was seen in many circles for many years as an arch-villain. He had ordered the courts martial and approved and signed the sentences. He had been absent—and it was suggested deliberately so—when attempts were made to lodge an appeal or to seek a stay of execution. And when he visited Australia in 1910 it was said that he refused to attend the unveiling ceremony of the Bathurst War Memorial unless Handcock's name was removed from it.

That story gained credence and by the time I came to write my novel it was firmly lodged in the national mind as a fact. I took it as such and wrote of it in those terms, for which I now apologise to the ghosts of Kitchener and the Bathurst worthies concerned.

Recent research has shown clearly that Handcock's name was one

Lieutenant P. J. Handcock's son, Peter, taken after Handcock's name had been placed on the Boer War Memorial at Bathurst

of many omitted by committees appointed to deal with memorial matters. In 1904, for example, after an exchange of letters and references the Town Clerk of Bathurst wrote to Mrs I. M. Howard:

'Dear Madam,

At last meeting of Council your letter stating the name of the late QMS Alan A. Howard had been left off the War Memorial, was considered.

Council recently decided to add another name to the Memorial and as there is room for one more name, it was decided to add the name of your late Husband.

I am directed to point out that the names placed on the Memorial were prepared and placed on same by a Citizens Committee, and so not a concern of this Council.'

The efforts of the Handcock family in a later generation saw his name added to those on the Memorial for the first time. Whatever else Kitchener may have done he could not have insisted on its removal, for it was never there in his lifetime. As to things he may have done in the cases of the BVC men, well, certainly, there are some that can be looked at askance—his action on having the executions carried out so quickly, for instance, and his absence at a crucial time. He may, indeed, have bowed to covert or indirect pressures from London, or even from Berlin via London, but of that there is no proof that has ever been found. Like much in the strange, swinging, sad story of Breaker Morant there is some confusion and a deal of conjecture. Kitchener has gone into history as a masterful figure, a shape of grandeur and great honours, whose loss in the sinking of *Hampshire* in 1916 was widely mourned.

Morant has gone not so much into history as into legend. He followed the admired track of other Australian folk-heroes—Ned Kelly, Moondyne Joe, Captain Starlight. They were all men against authority; good bad men or bad good men, always with enough human appeal to disguise the fact that they were outside the law, that they robbed and killed and were brought to book. Behind them all are the near-mythic figures of Hereward the Wake and Robin Hood, of William Tell and the outlaws of the Old West. People *prefer* to think of them all as bold and brave individuals, self-reliant and strong, defiant against great odds. Morant, in the popular mind, has joined their company.

And in The Breaker's shadow, barely seen, there are the other spectral shapes: Handcock, the simple, loyal, and possibly murderous follower; the pale and unknown Picton; Witton, with his book as his memorial; Lenehan, the passive commander who fought like a tiger for his good name; the slippery Taylor, gone into safety, perhaps with a bag of vanished gold; and the oddly-gaited, gaunt shape of Thomas, walking at night through the Tenterfield cemetery.

Perhaps now they may rest in peace.

A photograph of the grave of P. Handcock and Harry H. Morant (*Photo: Courtesy of W. H. Badior, J.P.*)

Select Bibliography

DENEYS REITZ. *Commando*. 1929.
PEMBERTON, W. B. *Battles of the Boer War*. 1964.
HOBSON, J. A. *The War in South Africa*. 1900.
HOLE, H. M. *The Jameson Raid*. 1930.
RAYNE KRUGER. *Goodbye Dolly Gray*. 1959.
JUDD, D. *The Boer War*. 1977.
CONAN DOYLE. *The Great Boer War*. 1902.
GRIFFITH, KENNETH. *Thank God We Kept the Flag Flying*. 1974.
FULLER, J. F. C. *The Last of the Gentlemen's Wars*. 1937.
WALLACE, EDGAR. *Unofficial Despatches*. 1901.
ABBOTT, J. H. M. *Tommy Cornstalk*. 1902.
CHURCHILL, WINSTON. *My Early Life*. 1943.
BUCHAN, JOHN. *Memory Hold the Door*. 1940.
WITTON, G. R. *Scapegoats of the Empire*. 1927.
CUTLACK, F. M. *Breaker Morant*. 1962.
CARNEGIE & SHIELDS. *In Search of Breaker Morant*. 1979.
SCHULENBERG, C. A. R. *Die Buishveldt Carbineers*. 1981.
LARKINS, W. R. *A Short Account of Loch's Horse*. 1902–03.
MONTGOMERY OF ALAMEIN. *A History of Warfare*. 1968.
MACKSEY, KENNETH. *The History of Land Warfare*. 1973.
PAKENHAM, THOMAS. *The Boer War*. 1979.
RENAR, FRANK. *Bushman and Buccaneer*. 1902.
BURLEIGH, BENNETT. *The Natal Campaign*. 1900.
JARVIS, C. S. *Half a Life*. 1943.
CHAMBERLAIN, W. *To Shoot and Ride*. 1967.
PATERSON, A. B. ('Banjo'). *Happy Despatches*. 1934.

Index

Ashton, Sergeant Walter 101

Barratt, Sergeant J. 127
Barton, Sir Edmund 136
Baudinet, G. W. 51, 131
Beyers, Commandant 105
Boers 17, 19, 24, 26, 29, 31–34, 36–38, 41–44, 47, 49, 87, 89, 90, 96, 99, 100, 101, 102, 133, 135, 147, 153, 154
Bolton, Major 98, 99
Bonham, Captain 104
Bonaparte, Napoleon 13, 24
Boony, Trooper, 98
Botha, General Louis 29, 41
Botha, Trooper Theunis 90, 96, 98, 103, 105
Breaker, The *see* Morant, Harry Harbord
Bright, Lieutenant 51
Bristow, Mrs 104, 112, 113
Brodrick, St John 114, 119
Buller, Sir Redvers 21
Burleigh, Bennet 81, 83
Burn-Begg, Captain 96
Bush Veldt Carbineers (BVC) 39, 44, 45, 48, 49, 50–52, 53, 54, 56, 58, 67, 84, 85, 86, 87, 89, 90, 91, 93, 98, 106, 114, 117, 122, 124, 130, 131, 134, 137, 139, 153, 154, 156

Calley, Lieutenant 23
Carter, Colonel 86
Chapman, Austin 141
Chauvel, Captain C. H. E. 61
Churton, Trooper 108
Copland, Major C. S. 96, 130
Court of Inquiry 85, 86, 90, 91, 100, 114, 139, 145
Court Martial 85, 89, 92, 94–117, 131, 134, 139, 141, 145, 146
Cradock, Colonel 100
Cronje, General Piet 41
Cutlack, F. M. 70

Dawson, Senator 141, 143
Dearden, J. F. 148–49
De la Rey, General Jacobus H. 29, 41
Dempsey, Mrs 123, 124, 126
Denny, Lieutenant-Colonel H. C. 96, 130
De Wet, General Christiaan 29, 41
Duckett, Trooper 99–100

Edwards, Lieutenant 51, 99
Eland, Sergeant Frank 89, 106

Finn, General 142, 143
Fisher, Reverend Canon 126
Forrest, Sir John 138, 139
Freehill, Major 143
French, Sir John 81

Garland, J. 128
Garrett, Colonel 101
Geyser, Mrs 153
Guy, Lieutenant B. F. 100

Haig, Colonel 44
Hall, Colonel 85, 97, 98, 106, 110, 112–13
Hamilton, Colonel 97, 110
Hammett, Sergeant-Major 54, 85, 100, 102
Handcock, Peter Joseph 10, 27, 51, 64–68, 85, 86, 87, 89, 90, 91, 92, 96, 98, 99, 100, 102, 103, 107, 108, 109, 110, 112, 113, 116, 119, 122, 123, 124, 126, 127, 129, 130, 131, 133, 134, 145, 147, 152, 154, 155, 156
Hannam, Lieutenant 51, 85, 89, 90, 100
Heese, Reverend Daniel 90, 102–03, 110, 111, 112, 113, 114, 133, 147, 153
Howard, Major 44
Hughes-Morgan, Major-General Sir David 86
Hunt, Captain Frederick 51, 84, 88–89, 96, 97, 98, 99, 101, 102, 105, 106, 107, 115, 126, 130, 136
Hutson, Captain H. D. 127
Hutton, Major-General Edward 57, 58, 135, 136–37, 138–39, 141, 142, 143, 144

Isaacs, Sir Isaac 133

Jameson, Dr Leander 19
Jennings, Edgar 150, 151–52
Johnston, Civil Surgeon Dr 98, 126, 127
Joubert, General Piet 41

Kelly, Commandant Tom 91, 100
Kelly, Lieutenant 50, 51
King, Captain 101
King, Edward 119
Kipling, Rudyard 74
Kitchener, General Horatio Herbert 9, 27, 29,

159

31–34, 44, 49, 93, 96, 97, 100, 109, 114, 119, 131, 133, 136, 144, 154, 155, 156
Krause, Reverend Oscar 110, 112
Kruger, President Paul 19, 24, 25, 29

Ledeboer, L. 96, 99, 105
Lenehan, Major Robert William 10, 51, 53, 56, 57–58, 63, 84, 85, 87, 88, 90, 91, 97, 98, 99, 102, 106, 116, 117, 119, 131, 134–45, 147, 154, 156–57
Levy, Captain J. N. 50, 51
Logan, J. D. 133
Longley, Captain J. R. 127
Lucas, Trooper 99–100

McArthur, Sergeant 101
Magee, Pat 78
Midgelly, Lieutenant 51
Milner, Lord 49–50
Morant, Harry Harbord ('The Breaker') 9, 10, 27, 46, 51, 57, 63, 68–84, 85, 89, 90, 91, 92, 93, 96, 97, 98, 99, 100, 102, 103, 105, 106, 107, 109, 110, 115, 116, 117, 119, 122, 124, 126–29, 130, 131, 133, 134, 136, 138, 145, 147, 152, 156; poetry 46, 74–77, 78, 79
Morant, Charles Ansell 69, 70, 71
Morant, Admiral George 69, 128
Morant, Mrs 128
Morrow, J. H. 124, 126
Mortimer, Lieutenant H. S. 51
Murrant, Edwin Henry 68, 71, 84

Neatson, Major 98
Neel, Dr 50, 51, 126

Ogilvie, Will 71, 78
Oldham, Sergeant 87, 107
Onslow, Colonel 142, 143

Parkes, Sir Henry 62
Phillip, Trooper 102
Phillips, Lieutenant Colin 101
Picton, Harry 10, 51, 52–54, 85, 89, 91, 92, 96, 97,
115, 116, 117, 122, 126, 127, 129, 130, 156
Poore, Lieutenant-Colonel 129–30
Powell, Trooper Edward 104, 107–08
Purland, Captain 63

Reader, Major 82
Reitz, Deneys 44
Reuter, Reverend F. L. 96, 98, 107
Rhodes, Cecil 17, 19
Roberts, Lord 27, 29, 32, 46, 57, 82
Robertson, Captain 86, 87, 88, 89, 96, 98, 99, 107

Schiels, Mrs 104, 112, 113
Schulenberg, Dr C. A. R. 94, 106–07
Sharp, Corporal 96, 103
Silas 110, 111–12, 113
Smuts, General Jan 41, 49

Taylor, Captain Alfred ('Bulala') 85, 86–87, 89, 92, 97, 98, 99, 102, 103, 107, 109, 112, 115, 116, 117, 126, 153, 157
Tennyson, Baron 139
Thomas, James Francis 10, 61–64, 94, 96, 113, 114, 117, 119, 130, 133, 134, 141, 145–52, 154, 157
Thompson, Trooper 99, 100, 103
Truman, Miss Hilda 70, 71
Tucker, J. E. 100

Van Buren, Trooper 88, 92, 99, 107, 108
Van Rooyen 103, 111
Viljoen, Field-Cornet 89
Visser, Josef 89, 92, 96, 97, 98, 104, 105, 106, 107, 115

Waddell, Colonel 143
Walters, W. P. 150–51
Witton, George Ramsdale 10, 51, 54–56, 68, 85, 86, 89, 90, 91, 94, 96, 98, 99, 100, 113, 114, 115, 116, 117, 119, 122, 129, 130–34, 141, 147, 154, 156
Wolseley, Sir Garnet 24
Wrench, Sergeant 100

THE DAILY TELEGRAPH.

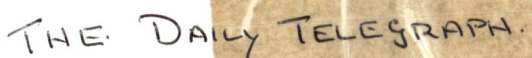

MAY 30TH. 1988

Soldiers 'cleared' of Boer killings

Two Australian soldiers sentenced to death by a British military court and executed during the Boer War have been acquitted in a retrial in period costume at Burra, north of Adelaide.

Lieut Harry Morant, subject of the film "Breaker Morant", and Lieut Peter Handcock claimed they were acting on orders when found guilty of shooting captured Boers. A recently-found diary recording Lord Kitchener's verbal instruction to "take no prisoners" was key evidence.